Contents

Section Two - Economic Awareness

Topic One - The National Business

Topic Two - Business Background

Topic Three - At Work

Section Three - Enterprise

Topic One - Business Activities

Topic Two - Accounting For Business

EDCO

BUSINESS STUDIES

REVISE WISE

JUNIOR CERTIFICATE HIGHER LEVEL

Cian Ó Grádaigh

Edco
Edco
The Educational Company of Ireland

This logo indicates material that you need to understand

 This logo indicates things that you need to be able to do

 This logo indicates exam questions

 This logo indicates a revision hint

Topic Three - Applied Accounts

Topic Four - Information Technology

Introduction

This book is intended to help you maximise your performance in the Junior Certificate Business Studies exam. By highlighting the main points of each topic, you can concentrate on the points needed to answer each question.

The Junior Certificate Business Studies Revision Guide is designed to be used alongside your exam papers and contains suggested solutions to many questions, particularly those that are asked often. It is not intended to replace your textbook, which will have fuller explanations and more examples.

The Course

The subject is divided into four sections, each of which is made up of a number of chapters in this book. Each chapter contains material that you need to *understand* and things that you need to be able *to do*. These are indicated by the logos:

 How to

 Understand

Many of the questions on Paper One, Section A are definitions of terms that we have asked you to 'understand'. Paper One Section B and Paper Two contain longer questions. Some chapters are examined more often than others and these chapters are highlighted in the Table of Contents by the symbol:

Exam Question

Sample Questions and Answers

Each chapter contains sample questions and answers that are designed to help you understand the material. If you practise the questions and understand how the sample answers have been calculated, then you will be well prepared for your exam.

Every time an exam question is referred to, it is written like this:

H '06 I B4(a)

Which means: Higher Level, 2006, Paper I, Section B, Question 4, Part (a).

The Study Plan

The study plan may help you to plan your work coming up to the examination.

- Write a list of all the topics you have to cover.
- Read and reread the text and then test yourself on what you remember. Do this by using points or spider diagrams

How to use your Study Plan?

- Plan the work schedule. Do not plan more than you feel you will achieve
- Keep to a daily timetable of work. Fill in the study plan for each day between now and the exam
- As you complete each task that you have set yourself, tick it off. This will make you feel you have made progress
- If you fall behind in your plan, don't give up! Start again!

Good Luck!

CHAPTER 1
Income

●●●**Learning Objectives**

Learn how to:
- complete payslips

Understand:
- sources of income
- benefit-in-kind
- statutory deductions: PAYE and PRSI
- voluntary deductions
- gross pay
- net pay

Tip

Tick each one off when you feel confident that you know it.

Understand

Income

Income is money earned. It can be either of the following:
- **Regular** income is paid at fixed intervals, e.g. unemployment benefit, wages or salary
- **Additional** income is received occasionally, e.g. bonus, overtime or a commission
- **Benefit-in-kind** is also a form of income, sometimes known as a 'perk' and is not paid in the form of money. The benefit can be official, e.g. company car, discounted insurance, or unofficial, e.g. personal phone calls, stationery.

The following table shows the main sources of income for people in different circumstances.

Student	Employed	Self-employed	Unemployed
Pocket money	Salary/wages	Profit from business	Unemployment Benefit
Part-time work	Benefit-in-kind		Family Income Supplement
Grant	Bonus		

Deductions

Statutory deductions are what you must give up from your salary/wages. They are:

- **PAYE** (**P**ay **A**s **Y**ou **E**arn), i.e. income tax
- **PRSI** (**P**ay **R**elated **S**ocial **I**nsurance), i.e. a contribution towards future State-paid Social Welfare Benefits (social welfare pension, sickness benefit, health care, unemployment benefit)

Voluntary deductions are what you *choose* to have paid from your salary/wages, e.g. pension contribution, health insurance, trade union subscription.

Payslip

Everyone who is employed must get a payslip that shows their name, the period covered by the payslip, the **gross pay** and all the deductions that have been made to it, and the **net pay** (i.e. the take-home pay). Payslips are referred to as wage slips in some cases.

Gross pay (gross wage)

- basic pay + overtime + commission + bonus = gross pay

Net pay (net wage)

- gross pay – all deductions (i.e. both statutory and voluntary) = net pay

Sample Question

O '02 B4 (excerpt only)

Mary Whyte is employed as a sales assistant in a large store. Her normal working week is 36 hours. If she works any longer, she gets overtime pay at time-and-a-half.

Last week Mary worked 40 hours. Her PAYE was €39.55 and her PRSI was €19.95.

Her employer deducts €25 each week from her wages for a savings scheme. Using this information, complete her wage slip for Week 11, dated 15 March 2002.

NB In a previous part of the question (not shown) you were asked to calculate Mary's hourly pay. The answer is €7 per hour.

Answer

Wage Slip: Mary Whyte			Week 11	
PAY	€	DEDUCTIONS	€	
BASIC	252.00	PAYE	39.55	
OVERTIME	42.00	PRSI	19.95	
		SAVINGS	25.00	NET PAY
GROSS PAY	294.00	TOTAL DEDUCTIONS	84.50	209.50

Workings

36 hours at €7 per hour = 36 x 7 = €252.00
40 – 36 = 4 hours overtime
7 x 1½ = €10.50
4 x €10.50 = €42.00 overtime pay

Total deductions €39.55 + €19.95 + €25.00 = €84.50
€294.00 – €84.50 = €209.50

Tip

In most questions where you have to work something out, you will lose marks if you do not write out the sum you did, even if you work it out with a calculator.

Exam questions on payslips may be combined with a question on the Wages Book (see chapter 20).

Questions

Try these other questions

H '04 I B6(a)   H '03 I B6(b)   H '02 I B4(a)

H '00 I B6(c)   H '98 I A4   H '06 I B4(6) iii

Learn how to:

● calculate a bill, e.g. from the ESB

Understand:

● current expenditure
● capital expenditure
● irregular expenditure
● discretionary expenditure
● opportunity cost

Tip

Tick each one off when you feel confident that you know it.

Understand

Expenditure

Current Expenditure (known in business as revenue expenditure) is spent on goods and services for immediate use, e.g. ESB bill, buying food, a holiday.

Capital Expenditure is spent where we will continue to enjoy the benefits in the future, e.g. buying a house or a car, getting the house rewired.

Fixed Expenditure is the term used for bills which have to be paid regularly, with the amounts usually known in advance e.g. mortgage repayments.

Irregular Expenditure is spent on bills, which have to be paid regularly, but the amount varies each time.

Discretionary Expenditure is spent on things that are entirely optional, e.g. eating out in a restaurant.

See page 13 for further details.

Sample Question

Put the following terms in the following table to show if they are fixed, irregular or discretionary expenditure.

Rent, Insurance, presents, magazine, clothes, mortgage, phone bill, groceries, holiday, entertainment.

Answer

Fixed	Irregular	Discretionary
Rent	Insurance	Presents
Mortgage	Phone bill	Holiday
	Groceries	Entertainment
	Clothes	Magazine

Opportunity Cost

The money price paid is not the only cost to the consumer. We all have a limited income, so we have to make choices. When we decide to buy something, we also decide not to buy something else. You sacrifice one thing to buy another.

Example: You go to a shop with €1. You choose to buy an apple instead of a packet of sweets. The packet of sweets you *did not buy* is the opportunity cost.

Sample Question

O '02 A5

Put a tick in the appropriate column in the table below to show if each item is Capital or Current Expenditure.

Answer

	Capital Expenditure	Current Expenditure
Rent		✓
Heating Oil		✓
New Washing Machine	✓	
Double Glazing	✓	
Phone Bill		✓
Phone Upgrade	✓	
Groceries		✓

How to

ESB Meter

One of the skills you need to be able to show is how to calculate an ESB bill from given information.

The **Standing Charge** is a fixed cost to pay for the wires coming to the house and must be paid even if you use no electricity.

Sample Question

O '98 A16

The following are meter readings taken from an ESB bill. Calculate the number of units used and the total ESB bill.

ESB Meter Readings

Present	49355
Previous	48765
Cost per Unit	€0.08
Standing Charge	€12.50

Answer

Workings

Number of Units:

49355 - 48765 = 590

Cost of Electricity

590 x €0.08 =   €47.20

add standing charge

                       €12.50

Total ESB Bill   €59.70

Tip

Many questions ask you to do more than one thing. You invariably need to do them in the order you are asked.

Questions

Try these other questions

Types of Expenditure

H '04 I A17

Dylan had €1 pocket money and was undecided whether to spend it on a bar of chocolate or a can of orange. He eventually bought the bar of chocolate.

(i) What was the opportunity cost involved? ....

(ii) What was the financial cost involved? ....

H '03 I A1

Indicate by means of a tick (✓) whether each of the following payments by a business would be regarded as Revenue Expenditure or Capital Expenditure.

	Revenue Expenditure	Capital Expenditure
New furniture		
Telephone calls		
Copying paper		
Computers		

O '02 A4

Complete the following sentence:

Impulse buying means...

Sample Questions

Meter reading

O '01 A4

The following are meter readings taken from an ESB bill. Calculate the number of units used and the total charge. Enter your answers in the appropriate spaces.

ESB Meter Readings

Present	47685
Previous	46895
No. of Units Used	
Rate per Unit	€0.09
Total Charge	

Answer

Workings

Number of units used = 47685 - 46895 = 790

Total Charge = 790 x €0.09 = €71.10

O '98 A 16

ESB Meter Readings

Present	274356
Previous	273487
No. of Units Used	
Rate per Unit	€0.15
Total Charge	

Workings

Number of units used = 274356 - 273487 = 869

Total Charge = 869 x €0.15 = €130.35

CHAPTER 3
Household Budget

●●● **Learning Objectives**

Learn how to:

- complete a household budget
- prepare a budget comparison statement

Understand:

- surplus
- deficit

Tip

Tick each one off when you feel confident that you know it.

Understand

Budget: A plan which estimates future income, expenditure and savings. A budget is a forecast.

How to

Steps to take in forming a budget:

1 Estimate income from all sources including overtime, social welfare, etc Include expected increases
2 Estimate expenditure. Divide into fixed, irregular and discretionary
3 Compare income with expenditure
4 Deficit = estimated income < estimated expenditure
5 Surplus = estimated income > estimated expenditure (this goes into savings)

9

Tip

When doing a budget question, pay attention to the following points:

- Make sure all information given is used in your answer.
- Where a figure changes from month to month, be sure that you enter the changes correctly, for example:
  - ➤ 'a bonus in October' means in October **only**.
  - ➤ 'will increase by €50 per month from November' means an extra €50 in November and every month after that.
- '€660 per year, payable monthly' means 1/12th, i.e. (660 ÷ 12 = 55) every month.
- As with any question with numbers, take care when writing. Keep your work neat by having the units, tens, hundreds, etc. aligned above each other. This reduces the risk of making a mistake in the sum.
- After completing the budget, there are generally a few extra questions. These are usually linked to the budget that you have just worked out.

Your revision notes

Sample Question

O '03 B1

Answer (A), (B) and (C). This is a Household Budget Question.
The following is a budget for the Byrne household for the last four months of 2003.
Opening cash in hand is €960.

Planned Income	Liam Byrne earns €2,500 net per month and expects to receive a bonus of €800 net in October.
	Carol Byrne earns €2,750 net per month and expects to receive a Christmas bonus of €500 net in December.
	Child benefit is €530 net per month.
Planned Expenditure	The house mortgage of €950 per month will increase by €50 per month from 1 November.
	• the house insurance premium, €660 **per year**, is payable **monthly** from September
	• Liam's annual car insurance is €785. Carol's annual car insurance is €640. Both are payable in October
	• household expenses are usually €1,200 per month except in December, when they are €1,000 **extra**
	• car running costs will be €250 per month for Liam and €295 per month for Carol
	• school books for the family will cost €800 in September
	• ESB bills are expected to amount to €340 in October and €570 in December, while a fill of heating oil, costing €850, will be needed in November
	• telephone bills for the home are expected to be €250 in September **and** November, while bills for mobile phones for all the family will be €195 per month
	• presents for birthday parties will cost €300 in September and €500 in October, while Christmas presents in December will cost €3,000
	• entertainment will cost €600 each month except in December, when it will cost €950 **extra**

(A) Complete fully the blank household budget form using all the above figures. (50)

(B) Explain what 'House Mortgage' means. (5)

(C) The Byrne family have purchased tickets for the All-Ireland Football Final. State whether this expenditure is fixed, irregular or discretionary. (5)

Answer

(A)

BYRNE FAMILY	Sep	Oct	Nov	Dec	Total
PLANNED INCOME	€	€	€	€	€
Liam Byrne's Salary	2,500	3,300	2,500	2,500	10,800
Carol Byrne's Salary	2,750	2,750	2,750	3,250	11,500
Child Benefit	530	530	530	530	2,120
(A) TOTAL INCOME	5,780	6,580	5,780	6,280	24,420

Fill in the figures supplied for each month. Be sure to include all details, e.g. Liam's €800 bonus in October is added to his salary for that month.

The Total column is calculated by adding across.

The **TOTAL INCOME** line is calculated by adding all of the Totals down for each month. The full Total in the bottom right-hand corner can be calculated by adding down or across. Use it as a way of cross-checking your sums.

(i)

PLANNED EXPENDITURE	Sep	Oct	Nov	Dec	Total
Fixed	€	€	€	€	€
House Mortgage	950	950	1,000	1,000	3,900
House Insurance	55	55	55	55	220
Car Insurance		1,425			1,425
Subtotal	1,005	2,430	1,055	1,055	5,545

All expenditure can be classified as FIXED, IRREGULAR or DISCRETIONARY. **Fixed Expenditure** is money you have to spend, where you know how much you have to pay and when you will have to pay it.

The subtotal is the total for **Fixed Expenditure** only.

(ii)

Irregular	Sep	Oct	Nov	Dec	Total
	€	€	€	€	€
Household Expenses	1,200	1,200	1,200	1,300	4,900
Car Running Costs	545	545	545	545	2,180
School Books	800				800
Light and Heat		340	850	570	1,760
Telephone Costs	445	195	445	195	1,280
Subtotal	2,990	2,280	3,040	3,610	10,920

Irregular Expenditure is money you have to spend, but either you do not know how much you will have to pay or when you will have to pay, e.g. you know when you will get the bill for the landline telephone, but not how much it will cost; you know how much credit for a mobile will cost, but not when you will have to buy it.

(iii)

Discretionary	Sep	Oct	Nov	Dec	Total
	€	€	€	€	€
Presents	300	500		3,000	3,800
Entertainment	600	600	600	1,550	3,350
Subtotal	900	1,100	600	4,550	7,150

Discretionary Expenditure is spending which you choose to make. This is the first to be cut when a there isn't enough money to cover expenditure (Deficit).

(B) TOTAL EXPENDITURE	4,895	5,810	4,695	9,215	23,615
	€	€	€	€	€
Net Cash (A – B)	885	770	1,085	–2,935	805
Opening Cash	960	1,845	2,615	3,700	960
Closing Cash	1,845	2,615	3,700	765	1,765

The **Total Expenditure** is calculated by adding the three subtotals (i), (ii) and (iii) above.

Understand

Net Cash

The difference between Total Income and Total Expenditure in each month is Net Cash.

i.e. TOTAL INCOME – TOTAL EXPENDITURE = NET CASH

If Expenditure is greater than Income, use a minus sign before the figure for net cash.

Opening Cash

The money the household has at the start of the month is the Opening Cash.

The Opening Cash in the TOTAL column is the same as the Opening Cash in the first month.

Closing Cash

The money the household has at the end of the month is the Closing Cash. Net Cash + Opening Cash = Closing Cash. This month's Closing Cash is next month's Opening Cash.

The Closing Cash in the TOTAL column should be the same as the Closing Cash in the final month.

If Total Income is greater than Total Expenditure, this is called a **SURPLUS**.

If Total Income is less than Total Expenditure this is called a **DEFICIT**.

The part of the budget that might cause some difficulty is the final section (Net Cash, Opening Cash, Closing Cash). The following question will help you practise these.

Sample Question

Adapted from H '02 I B1

Below is a partially completed summary of the O'Leary family budget for the months January to April. You are required to complete this budget by filling in the figures in the Total column and also the missing figures for Net Cash, Opening Cash and Closing Cash. On 1 January, the O'Leary family had cash in hand of €127.

Answer

	Jan	Feb	Mar	Apr	Total
	€	€	€	€	€
Total Income	1,250	1,250	1,350	1,375	5,225
Total Expenditure	975	1,538	1,521	1,179	5,213
Net Cash	275	–288	–171	196	12
Opening Cash	127	402	114	–57	127
Closing Cash	402	114	–57	139	139

Workings

Opening Cash, January €127

1,250 + 1,250 + 1,350 + 1,375 = € 5,225 (TOTAL INCOME)

1,250 - 975 = €275 (and so on for other months)

275 + 127 = €402

Partially Completed Budget

In this next question, you are given a partially completed budget to finish. You need to be careful in calculating the April–December estimate, making sure that you include the correct number of months and the correct sum for each month. It is probably easiest to do this in your Rough Work.

Tip

Remember to hand up all Rough Work and Workings. If you get it right in your Rough Work and Workings, but enter the figure incorrectly in the budget, you may still get some of the marks.

Sample Question

H '03 I B1

Answer (A) and (B). This is a Household Budget Question.   (30)

(A) On the next page is a partially completed personal Budget form for the Plunket family for 2003. You are required to complete this form by filling in the figures for the 'Estimate April to December' column, and the 'Total for year' column. The following information should be taken into account:

● Joseph expects to earn an extra €120 in overtime in October and November and will get a holiday bonus of €400 in June 2003

● Máire is going job sharing from 1 October and this will result in a 40% reduction in her salary from that date

● child benefit will increase to €110 per month from 1 July 2003

● the house mortgage will be paid off in full following the September payment

● car insurance is payable monthly and, from 1 September, it will increase to €50 per month

● household expenses will remain at the same level until the end of September and will increase by 10%, beginning in October 2003

● car running costs are expected to remain at €90 a month, with an additional cost of €160 in July for new tyres, and a car service will cost €130 in November 2003

● ESB for the 12 months Jan–Dec 2003 is estimated at €680

● the telephone bill is paid every second month and it is estimated that the cost will remain at the same level as at the beginning of the year

● a wedding present in May is expected to cost €130 and Christmas presents to cost €280 in December

● entertainment will average €180 per month for the remaining 9 months of the year

● a family holiday in July is expected to cost €1,500.

Answer

Plunket Household	Jan	Feb	Mar	Total Jan–Mar	Estimate Apr–Dec	Total for year Jan–Dec
PLANNED INCOME	€	€	€	€	€	€
Joseph's Salary	900	900	900	2,700	*8,740*	*11,440*
Máire's Salary	1,200	1,200	1,200	3,600	*9,360*	*12,960*
Child Benefit	100	100	100	300	*960*	*1,260*
A. TOTAL INCOME	2,200	2,200	2,200	6,600	*19,060*	*25,660*
PLANNED EXPENDITURE						
Fixed	€	€	€	€	€	€
House Mortgage	735	735	735	2,205	*4,410*	*6,615*
Car Insurance	40	40	40	120	*400*	*520*
Annual Car Tax		315		315		*315*
Annual House Insurance			385	385		*385*
Subtotal	775	1,090	1,160	3,025	*4,810*	*7,835*
Irregular	€	€	€	€	€	€
Household Expenses	810	810	810	2,430	*7,533*	*9,963*
Car Running Costs	90	90	90	270	*1,100*	*1,370*
Light and Heat	140		120	260	*420*	*680*
Telephone Costs		155		155	*775*	*930*
Subtotal	1,040	1,055	1,020	3,115	*9,828*	*12,943*
Discretionary	€	€	€	€	€	€
Presents	180			180	*410*	*590*
Entertainment	150	150	150	450	*1,620*	*2,070*
Holidays					*1,500*	*1,500*
Subtotal	330	150	150	630	*3,530*	*4,160*
B TOTAL EXPENDITURE	2,145	2,295	2,330	6,770	*18,168*	*24,938*
Net Cash (A – B)	55	–95	–130	–170	*892*	*722*
Opening Cash	120	175	80	120	*–50*	*120*
Closing Cash	175	80	–50	–50	*842*	*842*

Budget Comparison Statement

This question asks you to compare the Budget (remember it is a prediction) with what actually happened.

Clear instructions are given as to how the information is to be presented. Students who failed to follow the instructions in the question and left out the plus (+) and minus (−) signs lost valuable marks.

Sample Question

H '01 I B1(a)

Answer all sections. This is a Household Budget Question.

When the Doyle family checked their Analysed Cash Book at the end of December 2000, they found that their actual income and expenditure for the 12 months differed from the budgeted figures (contained in the Budget Comparison Statement on the next page) due to the following:

- Their salaries had increased by 10% from 1 July
- Child Benefit had increased by €10 per month from 1 April for each of the two children in the family
- The actual interest received was €37 less than budgeted
- They had won a prize of a holiday in USA which they did not wish to use and sold it for €1,200
- The mortgage had increased by €55 per month from 1 March and by another €25 per month from 1 November
- They had lost their no-claims bonus of €240 on their car insurance due to a car crash during the year
- House insurance costs were 20% higher than budgeted
- Household costs were 12½% less than budgeted
- The cost of shoes and clothes amounted to €1,635
- They had changed their car so that car costs had increased by €4,270 over those budgeted
- A saving of 8% had been made on the light and heat budget
- The only medical expenses for the year had resulted from monthly medication of €25 for the last three months of the year
- Entertainment costs had averaged €60 per month
- Gifts were €20 less than budgeted.

1 (A) Using the Budget Comparison Statement provided on the next page, enter the appropriate figures in the 'actual' column.

Then show the differences between the 'actual' and 'budget' figures by completing the column marked 'Difference'.

Use a plus or minus sign in front of each figure in that column.

Note: Use a plus sign if 'actual' is GREATER than the 'budget' figure.
Use a minus sign if 'actual' is LESS than the 'budget' figure.

Example

	Budget €	Actual €	Difference €
	430	480	+50
	780	710	−70
Total	1,210	1,190	−20

Answer

Income	Budget € Jan–Dec	Actual €	Difference €
Salaries	18,000	18,900	+900
Child Benefit	960	1,140	+180
Interest	150	113	−37
Other		1,200	+1,200
Total Income	19,110	21,353	+2,243
Expenditure			
Fixed			
Mortgage	4,320	4,920	+600
Car Insurance	397	637	+240
House Insurance	170	204	+34
Subtotal	4,887	5,761	874
Irregular			
Household Cost	7,504	6,566	−938
Shoes and Clothes	1,740	1,635	−105
Car costs	1,500	5,770	+4,270
Light & Heat	1,800	1,656	−144
Medical Expenses	200	75	−125
Subtotal	12,744	15,702	+2,958
Discretionary			
Entertainment	1,000	720	−280
Gifts	200	180	−20
Subtotal	1,200	900	−300
Total Expenditure	18,831	22,363	+3,532
Net Cash: Surplus/Deficit	279	−1,010	−1,289

Revised Budget

In revised budget questions you are given a completed budget for a few months and then told that certain information has changed. Some of your answers will be supplied in the information, some will come from the supplied budget, and the rest will be a combination of the two.

Sample Question

H '04 I B1

On the following page is an original Budget and a revised Budget form for the O'Mahony family from July to September 2003. After preparing the Budget for July to September 2003, Mr O'Mahony was informed that he would be getting a promotion in his job. This would result in an increase in the family income, starting in July.   (30 marks)

The O'Mahony family decided to revise their Budget in view of the changed circumstances. You are required to complete the revised Budget form, taking the following into account:

- Mr O'Mahony's annual salary will be €28,560 net, payable monthly
- Ms O'Mahony decided to go job sharing, which would result in a 30% reduction in her net salary from the beginning of July
- The O'Mahony family decided to buy a second car by getting another loan. The total cost of this new loan, including interest, will be €12,000, repayable monthly over 4 years, beginning in August
- The insurance on the new car will cost €450 for the year, payable in full in July
- Household costs will be reduced by €80 per month immediately
- Car running costs will increase by 40% per month beginning in July
- They decided to take a holiday in July at a cost of €1,600
- They intend to postpone the house decorating until November
- All other income and expenses are to remain the same.

Answer

Workings

Mr O'Mahony's salary   €28,560 ÷ 12 = €2,380 per month

Ms O'Mahony's salary   €800 - 30% = €800 - €240 = €560

If you are given no new information, the figures remain unchanged.
(Child Benefit, Mortgage, House Insurance)

The car loan is for a **second** car, so it will be added to the existing repayments. Note the repayments don't begin until August.

Additional monthly repayments   €12,000 ÷ 48 (4 years) = €250

Car running costs   €115 + 40% = €115 + €46 = €161

	Original Budget €				Revised Budget €			
INCOME	July	Aug	Sep	Total	July	Aug	Sep	Total
Mr O' Mahony's Salary	1,700	1,700	1,700	5,100	2,380	2,380	2,380	7,140
Ms O' Mahony's Salary	800	800	800	2,400	560	560	560	1,680
Child Benefit	40	40	40	120	40	40	40	120
Total Income	2,540	2,540	2,540	7,620	2,980	2,980	2,980	8,940
EXPENDITURE								
Fixed								
Mortgage	500	500	500	1,500	500	500	500	1,500
Car Loan	230	230	230	690	230	480	480	1,190
Car Insurance		510		510	450	510		960
House Insurance			190	190			190	190
Subtotal	730	1,240	920	2,890	1,180	1,490	1,170	3,840

	Original Budget €				Revised Budget €			
Irregular	July	Aug	Sep	Total	July	Aug	Sep	Total
Household Costs	920	920	920	2,890	*840*	*840*	*840*	*2,520*
Car Running Costs	115	115	115	345	*161*	*161*	*161*	*483*
Light & Heat		60		60		*60*		*60*
Telephone	75		75	150	*75*		*75*	*150*
Subtotal	1,110	1,095	1,110	3,315	*1,076*	*1,061*	*1,076*	*3,213*
Discretionary								
Holidays					*1,600*			*1,600*
Entertainment	200	200	200	600	*200*	*200*	*200*	*600*
Birthday & Presents	40		40	80	*40*		*40*	*80*
Household decoration		175		175				*0*
Subtotal	240	375	240	855	*1,840*	*200*	*240*	*2,280*
Total Expenditure	2,080	2,710	2,270	7,060	*4,096*	*2,751*	*2,486*	*9,333*
Net cash	460	−170	270	560	*−1,116*	*229*	*494*	*−393*
Opening Cash	−100	360	190	−100	*−100*	*−1,216*	*−987*	*−100*
Closing Cash	360	190	460	460	*−1,216*	*−987*	*−493*	*−493*

Questions

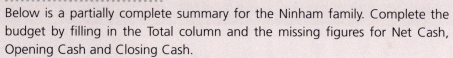

Try these other questions

Adapted from O '02 B1

Below is a partially complete summary for the Ninham family. Complete the budget by filling in the Total column and the missing figures for Net Cash, Opening Cash and Closing Cash.

On 1 January, the Ninham family had €256 in the bank.

	Jan €	Feb €	Mar €	Apr €	Total €
Total Income	2,040	2,040	2,600	2,244	
Total Expenditure	1,400	2,590	1,390	1,556	
Net Cash					
Opening Cash					
Closing Cash					

Try these other questions

Partially Completed	Budget Comparison Statement	Revised Budget
H '02 I B1	H '01 I B1	H '04 I B1
H '03 I B1	H '00 I B1	H '98 I B1
H '99 I B1		
H '06 I B1(a)		

●●● Learning Objectives

Learn how to:

- complete a cash account
- complete an analysed cash account

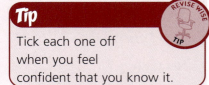

Tip

Tick each one off when you feel confident that you know it.

How to

Cash Book (record book 3)

Many households keep records in the Cash Book (record book 3) of money received and how money was spent.

The **Debit** (or Receipts) side is kept on the left-hand side and shows money in.

The **Credit** (or Payments) side is kept on the right-hand side and shows money spent.

Analysed Cash Book (record book 1)

The Analysis Columns are used to gather together expenditure on similar items such as groceries, light and heat or travel expenses.

Most households pay for some goods and services by cheque, while paying for other items with cash. The Analysed Cash Book may have two columns on each side: one for Cash, the other for Bank.
(Unused money columns on the debit side are not shown.)

Analysed Cash Book										
Debit (money in)					(money out) Credit					
Date	Details	fo	Cash	Bank	Date	Details	fo	Cash	Bank	Analysis columns

Tip

Debit side = Receipts = Money in
Credit side = Payments = Money out

The **Balance** is the amount of money left over at the end of the month and available at the start of the next month.
The Cash and Bank columns are balanced separately.

To balance the Bank column

1 Identify the column using the most lines (Debit or Credit side)

2 One line below the last entry, draw a line

3 Draw a line at the same place on the other side

4 Total the Bank column on both sides (debit and credit) but don't write anything yet

5 Write the bigger total below the line on BOTH sides

6 Put a double line beneath each total

7 Find the difference between each side

8 Write this difference above the single line on the side with the least amount of money and call it Balance c/d (c/d = carried down). The date for this is the last day of the week, month or year

9 Write the difference below the double line on the side with the most money. This is Balance b/d (b/d = brought down). The date for this is the first day of the next period (the next week or month usually)

10 Repeat the process for the Cash column

11 On the same line as the other totals (see point 4 above) write the totals of each of the analysis columns

Tip

The Cash column is balanced by the same method:
If the Balance b/d is on the DR (or Debit) side, you have money.
If the balance b/d is on the CR (or Credit) side, you have an overdraft.
You cannot have a CR balance in the Cash column.
The Balance b/d goes below the line on the side with the most money.

Sample Question

The Ward family keeps household accounts using an Analysed Cash Book. Mr Ward's salary is lodged directly into the bank and Mrs Ward's wages are paid in cash. During the first two weeks of April 2004, the family had the following transactions:

- they had a balance of €350 on their current account from last month
- they had €85 in cash
- they paid €55 for petrol (cheque 201)
- Mr Ward received his salary of €970
- Mrs Ward received her wages of €150
- they bought meat at the butcher's for €155 cash
- they went shopping for groceries, which cost €278 (cheque 202)
- a family day out at the cinema cost. €65 which they paid for in cash
- they paid the ESB bill of €85 (cheque 203)
- they had the car serviced, which cost €160 (cheque 204)
- Mrs Ward received her wages of €150
- they paid €80 for repairs to the lawnmower (cheque 205)
- groceries for the week cost €265 (cheque 206)
- Easter eggs cost €35 in cash

Write up and total the Analysed Cash Book of the Ward family for the two weeks ending 14 April 2004. Show the closing balance

Use the following money column headings:

- Debit (Receipts) side: Cash, Bank
- Credit (Payments) side: Cash, Bank, Food, Light & Heat, Car, Entertainment, Other.

Sample Answer

Debit

Date	Detail	fo	Cash €	Bank €
Apr-01	Balance		85	350
03	Mr Ward's salary			970
04	Mrs Ward's wages		150	
11	Mrs Ward's wages		150	
			385	1,320
15	Balance	b/d	130	397

Credit

Date	Details	fo	Cash €	Bank €	Food €	Light & Heat €	Car €	Enterta-inment €	Other €
Apr-02	Petrol	201		55			55		
04	Meat		155		155				
05	Groceries	202		278	278				
07	Cinema		65					65	
08	ESB	203		85		85			
09	Service on car	204		160			160		
12	Lawnmower repair	205		80					80
13	Groceries	206		265	265				
14	Easter eggs		35					35	
	Balance	c/d	130	397					
			385	1,320	698	85	215	100	80

Questions

Try these other questions

Analysed Cash Book

H '95 I B1

H '00 I B1

Tip

Note that a two-column (cash and bank) Analysed Cash Book has yet to appear on the Junior Certificate. But there is always a first time!

Your revision notes

CHAPTER 5

Informed Consumer

●●●**Learning Objectives**

Learn how to:

- calculate a unit price
- identify well-known symbols of quality and safety

Understand:

- consumer
- caveat emptor
- impulse purchase
- false economy
- deposit
- bar code
- loss leader
- price war
- symbols

Tip

Tick each one off when you feel confident that you know it.

Understand

Consumer

		For example
Goods	Things	Food, cars, houses, clothing
Services	Where you pay someone to do something for you	Hairdresser, car mechanic, entertainment

Caveat Emptor

The Latin expression *Caveat Emptor* means 'Let the buyer beware'. It is a warning to you, as a consumer, to spend your money wisely. It is your money and your loss if you do something foolish with it.

Informed Consumers know:
- their legal rights
- how to make a complaint
- what organisations are there to help and protect them

Informed Consumers buy with these questions in mind:
- Can I afford this?
- Is this the best price I can get?
- Do I need it?
- Does it do what I want it to do?

 **How to**

Unit Price

The best price is the lowest price, as long as the quality is the same. To compare different sized packages, calculate the unit price.
The lower unit price is the better value.

$$\text{Unit Price} = \frac{\text{Price}}{\text{number of units}}$$

Tip

The unit price is usually worked out in cents.

Sample Question

O'99 A6

Sláinte Cornflakes can be bought in two packet sizes, each a different weight and price.

Size	Weight	Price
Small	500 grams	€0.73
Large	1,000 grams	€1.50

Which is the best value for money?

Answer

Workings

Small $\dfrac{73}{500}$ = 0.146c per gram

Large $\dfrac{150}{1,000}$ = 0.15c per gram

The small packet has the lowest unit price. Therefore, it is the best value for money.

Understand

Impulse Purchase

When you buy something without having considered the purchase first, that's buying on impulse. This means that you will not have compared prices to find the least expensive one.

False Economy

There are two types of false economy:

1 Brand X costs €20 and Brand Y costs €40, but brand Y lasts three times longer than Brand X. To buy Brand X is a false economy because, in the long run, it will cost you more

2 A 500 ml bottle of Choke Orange costs €1.00. A 2-litre bottle of Choke Orange costs €2.50. The unit price of the bigger bottle is lower. It is a false economy to buy the bigger bottle but to drink only 500ml

Deposit

This is a small sum paid to the seller to hold the goods for you until you can afford to pay for them in full. If you do not come back within an agreed time, the seller can keep your deposit and sell the goods to someone else.

Bar code

A bar code is made up of a series of vertical lines and a thirteen-digit number. The bar code is made up of a country number, a company number, a product number and a check number.

ISBN 1-845-36044-3

9 781845 360443

Loss Leader

When a shop sells a product at a very low price to attract customers who will, hopefully, buy other goods once they are in the store, that product is known as a Loss Leader.

Price War

When shops selling similar products try to undercut each other to increase their market share, that is known as a Price War.

Symbols

A product may carry one or more symbols which give extra information to the consumer:

Symbol	Name	Meaning
guaranteed irish	Guaranteed Irish	Symbol of quality Irish goods
EIQA	Q mark	Symbol of quality Irish goods
WOOLMARK CERTIFICATION TRADE MARK	Woolmark	Product is made with pure new wool

Symbol	Name	Meaning
C E	CE mark	Product meets European safety standard
(Kitemark symbol)	Kitemark	Product meets British safety standards

Questions

Try these other questions

H '95 I B3(a)

Explain the following terms:

False Economy: _____

Impulse Buying: _____

O '01 1 A15

A consumer is:

a person who buys goods for resale	☐
a person who buys goods for business use	☐
a person who buys goods for private use	☐

Unit price:

H '99 I A18

Terms and definitions:

H '02 I B3 A(i,iv)

CHAPTER 6
This Will Not Affect Your Statutory Rights

●●●**Learning Objectives**

Learn how to:
- identify illegal notices

Understand:
- Sale of Goods and Supply of Services Act (1980)
- Consumer Information Act (1978)
- third party agencies
- proof of purchase

> **Tip**
>
> Tick each one off when you feel confident that you know it.

Understand

As a consumer, the law offers you some protection.

The Sale of Goods and Supply of Services Act (1980)

If goods (**purchased** or **hired**) or services are faulty, you have a valid complaint and are entitled to compensation.

Goods must be:
1 of merchantable quality
2 fit for their purpose
3 as described
4 according to sample

The supplier of any service should:
1 have the necessary skills
2 work with care and diligence

Any **parts** supplied should conform to points 1 to 4 above.

In all cases, it is the **seller** of the goods who is responsible for making compensation. This compensation may take the form of:

3Rs a) **full cash R**efund
b) **R**epair
c) **R**eplacement

The Act also makes the following points:

1. The seller and customer may **agree** to any of the above but the customer may **insist** on a cash refund
2. It doesn't matter how you pay; whether you buy, rent or hire purchase
3. The law still applies if you buy in a sale
4. A **guarantee** is a bonus offering you **additional** rights
5. It is illegal for a shop to display a notice which seems to limit these rights, for example:

No refunds during sale	Goods will not be exchanged
No liability accepted for faulty goods	Credit notes only

A **Credit Note** allows you to buy goods to a certain value in that shop.

Tip

If you buy **faulty** goods, you do not have to accept a credit note.

Proof of Purchase

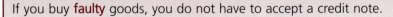

A **receipt** is the best proof that you bought the goods. You may need it when you make your complaint. If you pay by credit card, your credit card receipt, or even the bill, may be acceptable as proof of purchase.

The Consumer Information Act (1978)

This Act is intended to protect the consumer. It prohibits the following:
1 False or misleading:
  - claims about goods (e.g. that a product is unbreakable when it is not)
  - claims about services (e.g. that the premises is open twenty-four hours when it is not)
  - advertisements.
2 All statements about price must be accurate:
  - there should be no extra charge for items which should be included (e.g. if a product states 'batteries included', you shouldn't have to buy batteries separately)
  - VAT should be included in the displayed price
  - advertising false reductions in price is not allowed, e.g. if a good is priced at €149 ~~€199~~ (i.e. reduced from €199 to €149) it should have been on sale for €199 for at least 28 consecutive days in the past 3 months.

Director of Consumer Affairs

The Director of Consumer Affairs is responsible for investigating complaints made under either Act mentioned here.

EU and Food Labels

The European Union has laid down some more rules about the labels on foods:
1 What is it?
2 Who made it?
3 Where was it made?
4 Quantity (weight/volume and number of servings, where appropriate)
5 List of ingredients in order of weight
6 Best before/Use by date
7 Storage conditions (e.g. keep refrigerated, use within three days, etc.)
8 Instructions for use where necessary (e.g. cooking instructions).

Displaying Price on Food

All foods must display a selling price.

Food sold loose or in bulk (e.g. carrots) must display a unit price (usually per 100g or 1kg)

Third Parties

Where can I go for help with a problem?

If you have a complaint about an:	Go to the:
Advertisement	Advertising Standards Authority of Ireland
State-owned company	The Ombudsman
Insurance company	The Financial Services Ombudsman
Bank or other financial institution	The Financial Services Ombudsman
Holiday company	Irish Travel Agents' Association (ITAA)
Electrician	Registered Electrical Contractors of Ireland (RECI)
Car dealer/Garage	Society of the Irish Motor Industry (SIMI)
General consumer problems	Consumers' Association of Ireland (CAI)

Media

If you have a consumer problem and the shop is unwilling to talk to you, then radio shows such as *Liveline*, *The Gerry Ryan Show* and others may help by giving publicity to your grievance, or you could write a letter to your local or national newspaper.

Small Claims Court

If you cannot solve the problem any other way, it is possible to make a claim through the Small Claims Court. It will cost you €6 and you can make a claim up to €2,000. No solicitors are involved.

Questions

O '02 I A2

A consumer who returns a faulty good is entitled to either of **two** of the following:

Refund ☐

Revenue ☐

Repair ☐

H '06 I A16(a)

Joan purchased a pair of jeans in a shop which she did not examine closely until she arrived home. She found they were damaged. What form of redress is Joan entitled to? Explain your answer.

Try these other questions

H '03 I B5 (a,c)

H '02 I B3 (a,c)

H '00 I B5 (a,c)

H '99 I B4 (b)

Your revision notes

CHAPTER 7
Consumer Complaints

●●●Learning Objectives

Learn how to:

- identify valid complaints
- make a complaint
- write a business letter

> **Tip**
> Tick each one off when you feel confident that you know it.

 **How to**

Valid Complaints

A complaint is valid:
- if a good or service is **faulty**
- if an advertisement is false or misleading

Non-valid Complaints

A complaint is not valid:
- if you change your mind
- if there is a fault that was pointed out to you when you bought the item (e.g. if the goods were marked 'seconds')
- if the goods are damaged through misuse

Making a Complaint

The shop where you bought the item is responsible for putting things right. You must:
1. Contact the shop as soon as possible (in person, by phone or by letter)
2. Let them know what the problem is
3. Let them know what you expect them to do about it (remember the **3Rs**: **R**efund, **R**epair or **R**eplace)
4. Return the item
5. If you cannot reach an agreement, consult a third party

> **Tip**
> In the exam you are often asked to write a letter of complaint.

(39)

Writing a Business Letter

Tips

Letter-Writing Tips

- Write clearly
- Use the correct layout. Marks will be lost if you do not keep to the standard layout
- Give details of your complaint
- Include a **copy** of your receipt or other proof of purchase (keep the original in case the letter gets lost)
- Say what remedy you want (Refund, Repair, Replace)
- Keep a copy of the letter along with the original receipt

Sample Question

H '99 I B4(a)

Last March, Maeve O'Sullivan, Rioscarring, Ardara, County Donegal purchased a new aluminium patio door from Allbrite Ltd, Church St, Letterkenny. She paid €100 deposit on signing the contract ordering the door. It was installed two weeks later by an apprentice fitter. She paid the balance of €450 by credit card at the offices of Allbrite Ltd.

After a week she noticed that the door did not seal properly and allowed wind and rain in. After two months the door developed spots of rust.

On 13 May last, she wrote to the Sales Manager of Allbrite Ltd, lodging a complaint and enclosing evidence of purchase. She outlined the problem, stated her displeasure and demanded an immediate resolution.

Assume you are Maeve O'Sullivan. Write the letter of complaint to the Sales Manager of Allbrite Ltd. (22 marks)

Your
address
goes
here
The date of the letter

The name and address
of the person
you are writing to

Re: a one line description of the problem

Dear Addressee

Use a name if you know who you are writing to, but use the surname (e.g. 'Dear Ms Murphy') rather than the first name. If you don't know the name of the person you are writing to, you can address the letter 'Dear Manager'.

What did you buy?
Where and when did you buy it?
What is wrong with it?
How do you feel?
What do you want done about it?
Include a copy of the receipt.

Yours sincerely

Your signature
YOUR NAME IN BLOCK LETTERS

Answer

Rioscarring,
Ardara,
County Donegal.

13-05-04

Sales Manager,
Allbrite Ltd,
Church St,
Letterkenny,
County Donegal.

RE: Faulty patio door

Dear Sir/ Madam,

In March of this year I bought a patio door from you. I paid a total of €550, which included installation of the door. I have enclosed a copy of my receipt.

One week after one of your apprentices fitted the door, the seals failed and the wind and rain started coming through. Two months later, I was horrified to see spots of rust on what is supposed to be an aluminium door.

I do not think the door was of merchantable quality and I doubt the apprentice had the necessary skills to do the job properly.

I am thoroughly disgusted with this door and expect to hear from you immediately to arrange a time when a replacement door will be fitted by a properly skilled craftsman.

Yours sincerely,

Maeve O'Sullivan
MAEVE O'SULLIVAN

Answer

22 marks were awarded as follows:

Maeve's address	⟶	1 mark
The date	⟶	1 mark
The addressee (to whom was she writing?)	⟶	1 mark
Opening salutation	⟶	1 mark
What was bought?	⟶	2 marks
Proof of purchase	⟶	2 marks
What was wrong?		
Poor seals	⟶	2 marks
Rust spots	⟶	2 marks
Unhappy	⟶	2 marks
Suggest a remedy	⟶	2 marks
Closing salutation	⟶	1 mark
Signature	⟶	1 mark
The letter itself gets another mark for just being there	⟶	1 mark
More marks are awarded for spelling, punctuation, grammar, and using paragraph breaks.	⟶	3 marks
Total	⟶	22 marks

Questions

Try these other questions

H '03 I B5(a)

H '98 I B2(a)

43

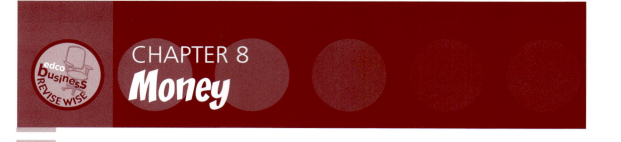

CHAPTER 8
Money

●●●**Learning Objectives**

Understand:

● forms of money (barter, legal tender, cheques, plastic (credit and debit cards), traveller's cheques, ATM)

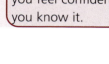

Tip

Tick each one off when you feel confident that you know it.

Understand

Barter

People exchange goods with each other, i.e. swap.

Money

Any token used in exchange for goods. This can take the form of coins or paper money.

Legal Tender

It is issued by the Central Bank and must be accepted as payment.

Currency

The official money of a country. In Ireland the currency is the Euro (€).

Functions of Money

1 Medium of exchange (used to buy things)
2 Measure of value (a way of measuring the price of things)
3 Store of wealth (a way of saving)

Features of Money

To work well, money must have the following features:
1 Portable (easy to carry)
2 Durable (it has to last; otherwise it won't work as a store of wealth)
3 Divisible (can be divided into smaller units to buy smaller things)
4 Confidence (people must believe it is genuine. They will not accept forgeries. A lot of money is spent on ensuring that currency is as difficult to copy as possible)

Other Forms of Money

Anything which performs the functions of money can be considered to be money. However, the only legal tender in Ireland is the Euro currency.
1 Currency (notes and coins)
2 Cheques
3 Traveller's Cheques
4 Credit Cards
5 Debit Cards

Question

0 '03 A9

Put a tick (✓) after each statement to indicate whether it is TRUE or FALSE.

	TRUE	FALSE
Barter means swapping or exchanging one product for another		
Legal Tender is a payment for a lawyer's advice		

●●●Learning Objectives

Learn how to:

- calculate interest on a deposit
- choose a financial institution
- open a current account
- prepare a bank reconciliation statement
- identify the best method of payment
- complete banking documents

Understand:

- reasons for saving and investing
- CAR, DIRT
- money transfer (Standing Order, Direct Debit, Paypath, Bank Giro)
- other banking services
- cheque guarantee card
- stale/blank/endorsed/crossed/post-dated/dishonoured cheques

Tip

Tick each one off when you feel confident that you know it.

 Understand

There are only two things you can do with your money: spend it or save it.

Saving = not spending.

Investing = putting your savings to work to earn an income called interest.

Why Save?

- to pay for something you can't afford right now (car, new bike, holiday, etc.)
- to provide an income for the future (pension)
- in case of unforeseen events (illness, loss of work, etc.)

People **Invest** to make a profit, i.e. get more money back than they put in.

How to invest

A wise investor will compare the possibilities and consider the following:

- Safety (high risk = low safety)
- Tax (DIRT)
- Interest
- Liquidity: how quickly can I get my money back?
- Convenience
- Other benefits, e.g. low interest loan, cheap insurance

 **How to**

Simple Interest

€ 1,000 is invested for 3 years at 10%

The formula is: Interest = $\dfrac{P \times T \times R}{100}$

P = Principal = sum saved
T = Time (years)
R = Rate of interest

$$\frac{1,000 \times 3 \times 10}{100} = €\,300 = \text{Interest Earned}$$

Your initial € 1,000 is now worth € 1,300

 **Understand**

Compound Interest

With compound interest, the interest is added to the principal so that you get interest on the interest. This means you get more interest in the long run. The **C**ompound **A**nnual **R**ate (**CAR**) is the rate you get when taking this into account. It is higher than the simple interest rate.

DIRT

DIRT stands for **D**eposit **I**nterest **R**etention **T**ax, which is a tax paid on the interest that you receive on your savings.

It is calculated as a percentage of the interest. DIRT is paid at 20%.

The Gross Interest was   € 300
DIRT, at 20%, would be   € 60
Net Interest received is   € 240

SSIA - Special Savings Investment Account

This was introduced in 2001 to encourage people to save. If you saved money every month for 5 years, the government added 25% to your investment. These accounts are no longer available.

Where Can I Invest?

A Commercial banks (AIB, Bank Of Ireland, Ulster Bank, National Irish Bank, Permanent TSB)

Deposit account (also known as a **Savings** account)

1   Money is deposited and can be withdrawn on demand
2   Interest is paid
3   You pay DIRT

A **Current** account (more flexible than a Deposit account)
1   Chequebook
2   Debit (Laser) Card
3   Overdraft (you can negotiate with the bank for permission to take out more money than you paid in, i.e. borrow money). You will pay interest on this
4   Most current accounts don't pay interest on the money held in the account.

B Building Society (Educational Building Society, Irish Nationwide, Building Society)

Deposit account

1   Limit on how much you can withdraw on demand.

C Credit Union

Savings account

1   When you save money you become a member
2   You get a share of any profit the Credit Union make
3   You do not pay DIRT on interest received
4   If a member dies, insurance will double the value of the deposit

Lending

1   Loans up to three times the value of shares held (i.e. savings)
2   If a member dies, insurance pays off the loan
3   The interest rate may be lower than the commercial banks

D Insurance Companies

Endowment policy

1   Fixed **regular** payments are made
2   After an agreed period (often 20 years or more) a **tax free lump sum** is paid out
3   Used to save for a pension or to pay off a mortgage

E An Post

Deposit account

National Instalment Savings Scheme (NISS)

1   Save a fixed sum each month for twelve months
2   The money is left on deposit for one to five years
3   The **longer** you leave the money in the account, the **higher** the interest **rate** paid
4   The interest is **tax free**

F Prize Bonds

1   Sold in units of €10
2   No interest is paid
3   Each bond is entered in a weekly prize draw
4   Can be cashed in at any time for the original cost

G Stock Market

Buy **shares** in a company

1   If you sell the shares, you may make a **capital gains** profit
2   The company may pay a **dividend**
3   **Capital Gains Tax** (CGT) is payable on any profit you earn
4   **Income Tax** is payable on dividends

You can also lose money if the price of the shares falls.

How to

Choosing a Financial Institution

	Safety	Tax	Interest	Liquidity	Convenience	Other Benefits
Commercial Banks	Yes	DIRT	Yes	On demand	Limited opening hours ATM	Mortgage Loans Other services
Building Society	Yes	DIRT	Yes	Limit on with-drawals Notice	Better opening hours (than commercial banks)	Mortgage
Credit Union	Yes	None	Dividend	On demand	Must go to own local branch	Loans Insurance on loans and deposits
An Post	Yes	Yes No tax on NISS	Yes	Limit on with-drawals Not possible with NISS	Many post offices open on a Saturday	–
Prize Bonds	Yes	No	No May win a prize	On demand	–	–
Insurance Companies	Slight risk	Not on Lump Sum	No	Difficult	–	–
Stock Market	Risky	CGT Income tax	Dividend	Sell any time	–	–

Sample Question

John had €5,000 to invest at 8% simple interest for 2½ years in a savings account which was subject to tax at 10%. Calculate the net interest earned. Show your workings. (7)

Solution

Gross interest = $\dfrac{5,000 \times 2.5 \times 8}{100}$ = €1,000

DIRT @ 10% = €100

Net interest = Gross Tax - DIRT = €1,000 - €100 = €900

Understand

Other Services

Apart from accepting deposits, what other services do financial institutions offer?

- strong room: valuables such as jewellery and important documents (e.g. the deeds to property) may be kept in the bank's safe or in a safety deposit box
- lending: a home loan is called a mortgage. A loan to buy something like a car is called a Term Loan
- Internet and telephone banking: pay bills and check lodgements
- advice: on saving money, investing, insurance, etc. Credit Unions give advice to members about balancing their household budget
- foreign exchange: banks buy and sell foreign currency notes

How to

Opening a Current Account

You will be asked to fill in a form and provide the following documentation:

- photo identification (e.g. passport, driver's licence)
- proof of address (e.g. ESB bill, phone bill)
- specimen signature
- new customers may be required to provide a reference, perhaps from an employer

 **Understand**

Operating a Current Account

Current accounts are used to make day-to-day payments.

Paypath: your pay is lodged directly into your current account by your employer.

The employer:
- does not need to have large amounts of cash on the premises
- does not need to take time to fill in cheques for each employee

The employee:
- does not have to take time off work to go to the bank

Making payments from a current account can be done by:
- Cheque
- Credit Transfer (C/T): to make a single payment to someone else's bank account, a **Giro** is used
- Bank Draft: this is a special form of cheque. It is drawn by the bank on its own account. Bank drafts are usually used for very large payments like buying a house. If you wish to send money abroad, a Bank Draft is the best way, as it is very expensive to negotiate a foreign cheque, even if it is a cheque in Euro
- Standing Order (SO): an instruction to pay a **fixed** sum into a bank account at **regular** intervals. Standing Orders are often used to make loan repayments or to pay rent
- Direct Debit (DD): permission given to a company to take money directly from the customer's account. Direct Debit is used where **the sum varies**, e.g. ESB bill, telephone bill

Tip

You need to know the difference between a Standing Order and a Direct Debit, and when to use each one.

How to

Bank Reconciliation Statement

Two sets of records exist which record your current account transactions:

Bank Account (in the Cash Book): your record of what you think is in the bank.

Bank Statement: a letter from the bank stating the actual amount in your bank account.

These should be mirror images of each other. If you lodge money, you enter it on the DR side of the Bank Account as it is something you own.

The bank will enter it on the CR side of your account as they owe you the money.

The bank account and the bank statement may show different balances because:

1 You made a lodgement after the statement date
2 A cheque you lodged was dishonoured
3 You wrote a cheque but the payee hasn't lodged it yet
4 Bank charges that you have not included in your cash book
5 Interest paid or received that you have not included in your cash book

You can change you own records if you get more information but you cannot change the bank's records.

If, after correcting your Bank Account, the Statement Balance and the Account Balance do not agree, you need to prepare a Bank Reconciliation Statement to explain the difference.

Steps to Prepare a Bank Reconciliation Statement:

1 Compare your Bank Account with the Bank Statement
  - Put a ✔ beside any item which appears on the Statement AND the Bank Account.
  - Put an ✕ beside any item which appears in the Statement only.
  - Put an ✕ beside any item which appears in the Bank Account only.
2 Update your Bank Account by including the items you've just marked with an ✕ on the Statement.
3 Complete the Bank Reconciliation Statement

Sample Question

Eoin Loftus has an account with Allied Irish Banks plc. He received the following Bank Statement on 2 May 2006.

Statement of Account
Allied Irish Banks plc
Dungarvan
County Waterford

Mr Eoin Loftus					
Lioscarrig			Branch code	93-21-33	
Ardeevin			Account No.	47190347	
Dungarvan			Date	01-May-06	

Date	Particulars	Debit €	Credit €	Balance €
2006				
01-Apr	Balance Forward ✓			589
03-Apr	Cheque 82 ✓	321		268
05-Apr	ATM Clonmel ✓	120		148
08-Apr	Paypath ✓		758	906
12-Apr	Cheque 85 ✓	271		635
13-Apr	SO – New Ireland ✕	520		115
15-Apr	Credit Transfer ✕		35	150
17-Apr	Bank Charges ✕	5		145
18-Apr	Cheque 84 ✓	719		574DR
20-Apr	Cheque 83 ✓	36		610DR
22-Apr	Paypath ✕		863	253
23-Apr	DD – ESB ✓	102		151
27-Apr	Cheque 86 ✓	120		31
30-Apr	Interest ✕	2		29

The following is Eoin's own record of his bank transactions. Compare his Cash Book/Bank Account with the Bank Statement he received. Make whatever adjustments are necessary to Eoin's Cash Book/Bank Account to bring his records up to date and prepare a Bank Reconciliation Statement at 30 April 2006.

DR		Cash Book/Bank Account				CR
Date	Details	€	Date	Details	chq. no.	€
2006			2006			
April			April			
1	Balance b/d	589 ✓	1	New TV	82 ✓	321
8	Wages	758 ✓	5	Grocer's ATM	✓	120
28	Lottery win	500 ✗	7	Entertainment	83 ✓	36
30	Balance c/d	142	8	MJ's Garage	84 ✓	719
			9	Oil	85 ✓	271
			20	ESB DD	✓	102
			24	Groceries	86 ✓	120
			29	Gorman's Stores	87 ✗	300
		1,989				1,989
			May-01			142

Tip

When comparing the Bank Statement and the Bank Account, pay attention to cheque numbers. The date of the cheque may differ; it is the number of the cheque that is important.

Answer

The updated Bank Account is shown below:

DR		Adjusted Cash Book/Bank Account				CR
Date	Details	€	Date	Details	chq. no.	€
2006			2006			
April			April			
	Credit transfer	35		Balance		142
	Wages	863		Bank Charges		5
				Interest		2
				Standing Order		520
				Balance c/d		229
		898				898
May-06	Balance b/d	229				

The Bank Reconcilation Statement always contains the same five lines:

Bank Reconciliation Statement at 30 April 2001		
Balance per statement		29
+ Lodgements not credited		500
		529
– Cheques not presented		300
Balance in Adjusted Bank Account		229

Lodgements not credited: anything on the DR side of the Bank Account that was not in the Bank Statement.

Cheques not presented: the total value of all cheques written (i.e. in the Bank Account) but not yet appearing on the Bank Statement.

Tip

Remember, the purpose of the Bank Reconciliation Statement is to explain any differences between the Bank Statement and the Bank Account. It starts with the Balance from the bank statement (the Balance on the last line of the Statement) and should finish with the Balance in the **Adjusted** Bank Account.

Methods of Making Payments:

- Cash
- Credit Card: a credit card allows you to buy goods up to a certain limit and pay for it altogether at the end of the month, e.g. Mastercard, Visa
- Charge Card: similar to a Credit Card. With a Charge Card you must clear the bill in full each month, e.g. American Express, Diners Club International
- Debit Card: Limited to the amount of funds available in your current account. The money is taken directly from your current account. It is like an electronic cheque, e.g. Laser
- Store Card: Like a credit card. You can only buy in a particular shop, e.g. Arnotts, Marks & Spencer, Statoil
- Postal Money Order: values from €15 to €650. A fee is charged as well. They are safer to send than cash in the post because the recipient has to sign it.
- Traveller's Cheques: they can be bought in various amounts and various currencies. You are required to show your passport when cashing them in, for security reasons.

Which to choose?

When considering the options available, bear in mind the following:
1. The cost to you and the recipient
2. Security: will your payment be safe from theft until the right person cashes it?
3. Convenience to you and to the payee (i.e. the person to whom you are paying the money).

Cheques

Your way of promising to pay someone from funds in your bank account.

The counterfoil or stub: your copy of the cheque payment. Use it to keep a record of your bank balance.

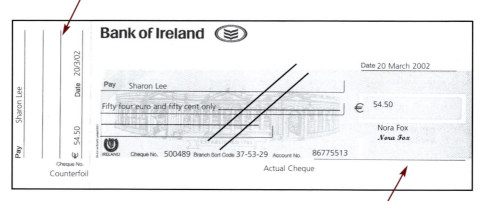

The counterfoil / Actual Cheque

The actual cheque: this is the portion you give to the payee.
When completing a cheque, bear in mind the following:
1. Write clearly
2. Begin the words and numbers as close to the left of the space as possible so there is no room to change the details that you write
3. It is best to draw a line through the remaining space for the same reason
4. Make sure that you put the correct date on the cheque
5. Never sign a cheque without filling in the rest of the details (i.e. never sign a blank cheque).

 **Understand**

Cheque Guarantee Card

When this card is presented at the same time as the cheque, the payee writes the guarantee card number on the back of the cheque. The bank guarantees to pay out on the cheque if it has a value less than €130 even if the drawer does not have enough money in their account.

You should never keep your cheque guarantee card and chequebook together.

Cheque Terms and What They Mean

Payee	The person receiving payment. Their name follows the word 'Pay' on the cheque.
Drawer	The person writing the cheque.
Drawee	The bank on which the cheque is drawn.
Negotiate a cheque	Bring it to a bank to get money for it.
Stale cheque	A cheque presented to the bank more than six months after it was written. The bank will not accept it.
Blank cheque	A signed cheque which has at least one piece of information left out, e.g. the payee or the value of the cheque.
Endorsed cheque	The payee has signed the back of the cheque so someone else can negotiate it.
Post-dated cheque	A cheque with a date in the future on it. It cannot be negotiated before that date.
Receipt cheque	A cheque that must be signed by the payee before it can be negotiated.
Dishonoured cheque	The drawee bank has refused to pay out on the cheque. Perhaps the drawer doesn't have enough money in their account.
Stopped cheque	The drawer has instructed the bank to dishonour the cheque.
Crossed cheque	Two parallel lines on the face of the cheque means the cheque must be paid into a bank account. Further instructions may be written between the lines.
Open cheque	A cheque that is not crossed.

Sample Question

Other banking documents

On 15 May 2004, Thomas Burns made a lodgement of €974 to the business current account. The lodgement consisted of a cheque for €650, notes totalling €310 and the remainder in coins.

Complete the lodgement form for the transaction of 15 May. Use the blank document supplied.

Answer

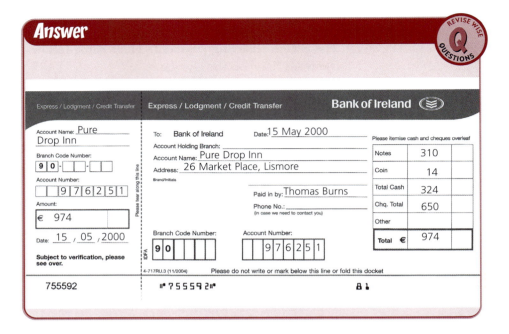

Questions

H '06 I A1

The following initials appeared on a bank statement. What do they stand for?

SO _____

CT _____

DO _____

ATM _____

Try these other questions

Interest	Banking documents & cheques	Bank Reconciliation	Saving and Investment	Miscellaneous banking questions
H '03 I A8	H '04 I B2(a)	H '01 I B3(b)	H '04 I A12	H '04 I B5(a)
H '02 I B2 (b,c,d)	H '03 I B2 (a,d)	H '97 I B3(e)	H '02 I B2 (b)	H '03 I B2(b)
H '06 I B 6B (i)	H '02 I A7		H '01 I A9	H '02 I B2(a,d)
	H '99 I A4			H '06 I B6(a)
	H '97 I A2			

●●●**Learning Objectives**

Learn how to:

- calculate cash vs credit cost
- apply for a loan
- match the period of a loan to the purpose

Understand:

- lending agencies
- collateral, security, guarantor
- short, medium, long term
- hire purchase vs deferred payment vs leasing/renting
- rights of the borrower
- cost of borrowing (APR)
- types of loan (overdraft, term, etc.)

Tip

Tick each one off when you feel confident that you know it.

How to

There are three ways to pay for something you wish to buy:
1 Cash (pay for it immediately)
2 Borrow (use someone else's money and pay them back later)
3 Credit (pay for it later)

Deciding to Borrow

Ask yourself four questions:
1 Do I need to borrow or can I wait and save up?
2 How much do I need?
3 What is the best option available to me?
4 Will I be able to meet the repayments?

Term

Money can be borrowed for varying lengths of time.

Short term	Less than 1 year	
	Overdraft	You take more money out of your current account than you put in to it.
		Interest is calculated based on the sum outstanding.
		Interest rates can be quite high.
		Used for financing day-to-day expenses (between paydays).
	Bridging loan	A short-term loan given to people who have been approved for a mortgage but have yet to receive the money.
Medium term	1 to 5 years	
	Term loan	You borrow money for a stated purpose and agree to make a fixed number of repayments at regular intervals.
		Interest is calculated on the sum borrowed.
	Personal loan	Used for buying a car, household furniture, etc.
Long term	5 years or more	
	Mortgage	You borrow money for a long time (20–30 years) in order to buy a house.
		The deeds to the house are used as collateral.
		Interest is calculated on the sum outstanding.
		Interest rates are much lower than for other kinds of loan.

Tip

The loan should not last longer than what you buy.

Understand

Source

The money can be borrowed from different sources:

Lending Agencies

- **Commercial Bank**

  Loans for many purposes and over varying terms
  - Overdraft
  - Term Loan
  - Mortgage
  - Bridging loan
- **Building Society**

  A wide range of loans but specialise in mortgages
  - Term Loan
  - Mortgage
  - Bridging Loan
- **Credit Union**

  You must be a member
  - Personal loans
- **An Post**
  - Term loans
- **Credit Card**

  Can be used to purchase items up to a certain limit which you pay for at a later date. The interest rate paid by the borrower is usually very high.
- **Pawnbroker**

  A pawnbroker will lend you money if you give them something valuable as collateral (e.g. jewellery). If you fail to repay on time, the collateral will be sold to repay the loan.
- **Licensed Money Lender**

  If you have difficulty borrowing money elsewhere, you may go to a money lender. Money lenders charge a very high rate of interest. (A licensed money lender may not charge more than 39% per annum.)
- **Unlicensed Money Lender**

  An unlicensed money lender is acting illegally.

Definitions

Collateral: Something of value given as *security* against a loan.
Security: Another word for collateral.
Guarantor: A person (often a parent) who promises to repay the loan if you do not.

Cost of Borrowing

The interest rate is the main cost of borrowing.

- *Flat rate of interest*: Interest is charged based on the full life of the loan. This is calculated as simple interest.
- *True rate of interest:* All other costs (administration, legal, etc) are included. If interest is calculated on the sum outstanding (declining balance), this is also taken into account. This is also known as *APR (Annual Percentage Rate).*

There may be other costs, such as legal fees, administration costs or insurance.

Buying on Credit

If you buy goods and pay for them at a later date, that is buying on credit.

1 **Deferred Payment** Payment is made in instalments. No interest is charged.
2 **Renting** You make regular payments in exchange for the use of something. You will never own it. You might rent a video from your local video store.
3 **Leasing** A special form of renting where you make payments for an agreed period. A student might lease an apartment.
4 **Hire Purchase** HP is a cross between deferred payment and leasing. You agree to make a number of fixed regular payments. While you are making payments the goods are not yours, but when you make the last payment you gain ownership. If you buy electrical goods from the ESB shop and pay for them on your bill, this is HP.

Comparison table

	Deferred Payment	Renting/Leasing	Hire Purchase
Ownership	From the start	Never	With final payment
Interest	-	-	Can be up to 25%
Can I give it back?	No	Only at the end of the term	When half the payments have been made

Rights of the Borrower

Whether you buy something on credit or borrow to buy it, you have certain legal rights:

1 Any advertisement for a loan must include the APR
2 The advertisement must also show the amount to be repaid. This may be shown as a 'cost per €1,000'
3 Advertisements for loans must tell you what may happen if you fail to keep up repayments
4 In the case of buying something on credit, you are always entitled to a Credit Agreement. This must show:
   a. the cash price
   b. the total credit price
   c. the number and size of each repayment
   d. if there is a deposit or 'Balloon' final payment, how much is it? (A Balloon payment is a final payment and is bigger than the regular instalment)
   e. a description of the goods
5 Any advertisement for HP must include the same details. It must also state who is offering the credit

 **How to**

Calculate the Credit Cost

Cash price:	€400
Credit price:	
Deposit	€50
18 monthly payments of	€25

$18 \times €25 =$ €450
€450 + €50 = €500

Tip

The *cash price* is what you would pay in cash.
The *credit price* is the total amount of money you pay including interest, the deposit and any charges.

Sample Question

Complete a loan application (OL'00B7)

Rhona King, who is single, lives at 56 Banks Road, Cork, in a house which she purchased in 1990 with the help of a mortgage of €40,000 from the Startup Building Society and to whom she repays €200 per month. Her telephone number is 021-134567.

Rhona is employed as a legal secretary with Smart & Keane, Solicitors, Airport Road, Cork where she started work in 1986. She earns a Gross Salary of €1,900 per month, out of which she pays income tax and PRSI totalling €650 per month.

Rhona wishes to buy a new car for her next birthday. She will be 35 years old on 14 August 2000.

In order to buy the car, she needs to borrow €10,000, which she hopes to repay in monthly instalments of €230 over the next four years. She is already paying the Cork Credit Union €50 per month for a loan of €1,000 which she obtained in 1999.

She gets a Loan Application Form from her local branch of AIB.
Complete Rhona's Loan Application Form as of today's date.   (40 marks)

Tip

Completing Forms

As with any form to be filled, it is important to give all relevant information accurately. The key to this is to read the question carefully and to tick off each piece of information as it is used.
It is also worth remembering that each space in the form needs to be completed.

Answer

REVISE WISE
QUESTIONS

LOAN APPLICATION FORM

PERSONAL DETAILS

Name	**Rhona King**	Mr, Mrs, Ms	**Ms**
Address	**56 Banks Road**		
	Cork		
	County Cork		
Number of years at this address	**14**	Owner or rented	**Owner**
Telephone	**021-134567**		
Date of Birth	**14 August 1965**		
Mortgage amount (if any)	**€40,000**		
Annual repayments on mortgage	**€2,400**		
Mortgage borrowed from	**Startup Building Society**		

EMPLOYMENT DETAILS

Occupation	**Legal Secretary**
Employer's name and address	**Smart & Keane, Solicitors**
	Airport Road, Cork
Net salary per month	**€1,250**
Number of years in your present employment	**10 years**

LOAN REQUIRED

Amount	**€10,000**
Purpose	**to buy a car**
How long do you want the loan for?	**4 years**
How much can you repay each month?	**€230**

Details of other existing loans

Lender		Amount		Annual repayments	
Cork Credit Union		Amount	**€1,000**	Annual repayments	**€600**
Signature	**Rhona King**		Date	**14 June 2000**	

Questions

Try these other questions

H '04 I A6	H '04 I B5(b,c)
H '03 I A5ii	H '98 I B4
H '00 I A2	H '97 I B4
H '00 I A3	H '06 I B6(c)

Your revision notes

●●●Learning Objectives

Learn how to:

- apply for insurance
- calculate premium
- apply the principal of contribution
- make an insurance claim
- calculate compensation with average clause

Understand:

- six principles of insurance
- insurable/uninsurable risk
- types of insurance (personal, property, motor)
- insurance vs assurance
- loading, discount
- actuary, loss adjuster, loss assessor
- premium, risk, compensation, days of grace

Tip

Tick each one off when you feel confident that you know it.

Understand

Insurance

Insurance is a way of protecting yourself against a financial loss that might happen.

Premium is the money you pay to buy insurance.

Compensation is the money the insurance company pays to you if you suffer a loss.

Risk is the accident that might happen:

1 *Insurable risk* Something which may happen and is beyond your control, e.g. a house fire, burglary, a car crash.

2 *Uninsurable risk* Some risks cannot be insured against, e.g. losses to a business due to bad management or damage caused by war or an earthquake.

How Insurance Works

Many people pay a premium

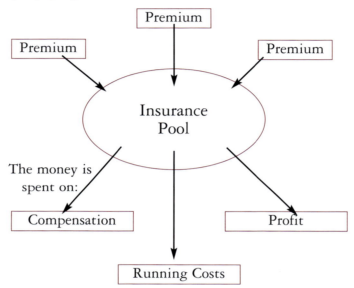

The 6 Principles of Insurance

Insurance is governed by a number of rules, known as Principles:

1 **Insurable interest:** You must be at risk of suffering a financial loss.

2 **Utmost Good Faith:** All information given to the insurance company must be true, complete and accurate.

3 **Indemnity:** You cannot make a profit from insurance.

4 **Subrogation:** If your insurance company pays you compensation, it can claim compensation from the person who caused the accident. If the insurance company pays compensation for damage, the insurance company then owns the damaged goods.

5 **Contribution:** If you have the same risk covered by more than one policy, the insurance companies will share the cost of the compensation between them. (See example on page 75.)

6 **Average clause:** In the case of under-insurance (less than full value), the insured will receive less in compensation than the value of damage done. (See example on page 75.)

Insurance Documents

Proposal Form: The form you fill in when applying for insurance.

Certificate of Insurance: The document the insurance company gives you. It details what is insured and what risks are covered.

Cover Note: Given if there is a delay in issuing the Certificate of Insurance. It is temporary evidence that insurance cover does exist. This is particularly important for motor insurance, which is required by law.

Policy: The policy details the conditions and exclusions to the insurance.

Claim Form: The form you fill in to seek compensation.

Days of Grace

Sometimes an insurance company will allow a few days for you to pay the premium after an existing insurance policy expires.

People in Insurance

The insurer: The insurance company.

The insured: The person getting insurance.

Broker: A broker gives advice to the customer and sells him/her insurance. A broker who sells insurance from more than one company is an *Independent Broker*.

Actuary: An actuary calculates the premium. Actuaries work for the insurance company.

Loss Adjuster: Calculates the value of the loss. Works for the insurance company.

Loss Assessor: Also calculates the value of the loss. Works for the insured.

Types of Insurance

Accident Insurance: Protection against an event that *might* happen. You pay a premium for a year and if an accident occurs compensation will be paid.

Life Assurance: Protection against an event that *will* happen. You pay an annual premium every year. If you are injured or die, or reach a specific age (usually 65), the policy matures (i.e. pays out). (You will definitely live to 65 unless you die first!)

Surrender Value of a Life Assurance policy is the money value of the policy if cashed in before maturity.

Motor insurance: Motor insurance is required by law.

In insurance, the owner is the first party, the insurance company is the second party and anyone else is the third party.

- **Third Party Insurance** This is the minimum required by law. Loss or injury to other people is covered, but the owner is not.
- **Third Party Fire and Theft** In addition to the cover above, if the vehicle is stolen or damaged in a fire, compensation will be paid.
- **Comprehensive insurance** Anyone involved in an accident is compensated, including the insured.
- **Pay Related Social Insurance** Covers loss of income from unemployment or illness.
- **Health insurance** (e.g. BUPA or VHI) Covers hospital bills, etc.
- **Travel insurance** Covers lost luggage, missed flights or illness on holiday.
- **Salary protection insurance** Provides an income if you need to give up work through illness or accident.
- **House insurance** Compensation for damage caused by fire or flood or loss due to burglary.
- **Public Liability Insurance** Compensation for members of the public injured while visiting your property.

Business Insurance

- **Motor insurance**
  Required by law.
- **Life insurance**
  For a sole trader to protect their family against loss of income.
- **Employer's Liability**
  Covers the cost of claims by workers injured at work.
- **Public Liability**
  Covers the cost of claims arising from damage to property and injury to individuals.
- **Product Liability**
  Covers the cost of claims by customers for injuries arising from using your products.
- **Goods in Transit**
  Covers the value of goods lost, damaged or stolen while being transported.
- **Fidelity Guarantee**
  Protects a business from loss due to dishonesty of employees.
- **Consequential Loss**
  Protects the business from loss of income due to fire, theft, etc.

How to
Applying for Insurance

Sample Question

Exam Question O '98 B4 (excerpt)

Margaret Perry, a teacher who lives at 25 High Road, Westport, wishes to insure her house and its contents for one year for €70,000. It is a detached concrete house in an area which has never flooded and it has never been damaged in any way since it was built.

Margaret and her family were never in any trouble with the law. She never had any problem getting insurance in the past. The only valuable articles she has in the house are jewellery valued at €2,000, a computer valued at €900 and furniture and clothing valued at €5,000.

Proposal Form for House and Contents Insurance
Gander Insurance Co Ltd, Race St, Castlebar

Name   *Margaret Perry*   Occupation   *Teacher*

Address   *25 High Road*

Westport

Insurance required from   *1 May 1998*   To   *30 April 1999*

Tick (✓) Yes or No in answer to each of the following

	Yes	**No**
1. Is your house i) built of stone/concrete?	☑	☐
ii) subject to flooding?	☐	☑
iii) detached?	☑	☐
2. Has your house been previously damaged?	☐	☑
3. Have you or your family		
i) been convicted of any crime?	☐	☑
ii) ever been refused insurance?	☐	☑

4. State how much cover you require

€   *70,000*

5. Apart from furniture and clothing, name any articles valued over €1,000

Jewellery €2,000

Signature: *Margaret Perry*   Date: *1 May '98*

Calculating an Insurance Premium (1)

Sample Question

The Brogan family wish to insure their house for €250,000 and its contents for €90,000. They receive a quotation from an insurance company of €8 per €1,000 for the building and €15 per €1,000 for the contents.

Calculate the total cost of the premium they would have to pay. Show your workings.

Solution

Building $$\frac{€250,000}{€1,000} \times €8 = €2,000$$

Contents $$\frac{€90,000}{€1,000} \times €15 = €1,350$$

Total premium = €2,000 + €1,350 = €3,350

 ## Understand

Discount and Loading

The premium is based on an average risk.

Discount: A reduction in the premium because you are a lower than average risk, e.g. your have a smoke alarm or a burglar alarm fitted.

No Claims Bonus: A discount for not having made a previous claim on motor insurance.

Loading: An increase in the premium because you are a higher than average risk.

How to

Calculating an Insurance Premium (II)

Sample Question

Éamonn was quoted €800 for car insurance. Because he is under twenty-five, a loading of 40% is to be added. When he told them the car would be kept in a garage at night, they gave him a discount of 10%. Calculate the premium Éamonn has to pay.

Solution

Basic premium = €800

Loading (age) = €800 x 40% = €320

Discount (garage) = €800 x 10% = €80

Total premium = €800 + €320 - €80 = €1,040

Tip

The loading and discount are both based on the basic premium.

Total premium is:
basic + loading - discount

Making an Insurance Claim

If an accident happens and you need to make a claim, you should get in touch with your insurance company. They will send you a **claim form** to complete.

Sample Question

Éamonn O'Doherty lives in 45 Owenstown Park, Baltinglass, County Wicklow. He owns a 1996 Ford Fiesta (98DL6138) of 1100cc. When he came out of the shopping centre in Gorey, County Wexford, he found his car was damaged. Someone had crashed into his car but did not stay at the scene. The driver's door was damaged.

He notified the Garda Síochána and they advised him to contact his insurance company and complete a claim form.

An estimate from his local garage says it will cost €550 to repair.

Complete the proposal form, giving today's date for the accident.

Answer

Motor Accident Claim Form

Insured

Name	*Éamonn O'Doherty*	Tel. (home)	*01-9851572*
		Tel. (work)	*01-2301964*

Address *45 Owenstown Park*
Baltinglass
County Wicklow

Date of birth	*7 May 1986*	Occupation	*Student*

Vehicle

Make	*Ford*	Model	*Fiesta*
		Engine	*1100cc*
Year of manufacture	*1998*	Registration	*98DL6138*

Accident

Full details of damage to the vehicle
Driver's side door damaged

Date of accident	*14-06-04*	Time of accident	*14:30*

Location of accident *Shopping Centre Carpark, Gorey, County Wexford*

Was anybody injured?   Yes ☐   No ☑
If yes, give details

Describe how the accident occurred
An unknown car crashed into mine in the car park.
The driver did not stay at the scene.

Were the Garda Síochána notified?	Yes ☑	No ☐
Were there any witnesses?	Yes ☐	No ☑

If yes, name and address of witnesses

Estimated cost of repair   *€550*

Driver

Name   *Éamonn O'Doherty*
Address *45 Owenstown Park*
Baltinglass, County Wicklow

Was the driver injured?	Yes ☐	No ☑
Was the driver arrested as a result of the accident?	Yes ☐	No ☑

Declaration

I declare that the above particulars are true, to the best of my knowledge.
Signed   *Éamonn O'Doherty*   Date   *14-04-04*

REVISE WISE QUESTIONS

Calculating Compensation (Average clause)

If you are fully insured, you will be fully compensated. In the example above, Éamonn would receive €550 in compensation.

If you are under-insured, the average clause will apply.

Question

A house is valued at €100,000 and is insured for €80,000.
Calculate the compensation payable if fire damage to the house amounts to €8,000.

Solution

$$\text{Compensation} = \frac{\text{Sum insured}}{\text{Market value of item}} \times \text{loss}$$

$$\frac{€80,000}{€100,000} \times €8,000 = €6,400$$

Only 80% of the house is insured, so the company will only pay for 80% of the damage.

Compensation (Principle of Contribution)

If you have the same risk covered under more than one insurance policy, each insurance company will share the compensation between them.

Question

Niall owns a laptop computer worth €1,500 which he has insured with Dial Insurance Ltd. His house insurance with Eblana Insurance Ltd also covers contents and will pay up to €1,000 for a single item. His house is burgled and his laptop is stolen.

a) How much compensation will he receive? Name the principle of insurance involved.

b) How much will each insurance company pay out?

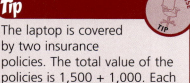

Tip

The laptop is covered by two insurance policies. The total value of the policies is 1,500 + 1,000. Each company will pay part of the compensation as shown below.

Solution

a) Niall will receive €1,500. The Principle of Indemnity says you cannot make a profit on insurance.

b) Dial Insurance Ltd will pay $\frac{€1,500}{€1500 + €1,000} \times €1,500 = €900$

Eblana Insurance Ltd will pay $\frac{€1,000}{€1,500 + €1,000} \times €1,500 = €600$

Tip

900 + 600 = 1500 this is the total compensation Niall will receive.

Questions

REVISE WISE Q QUESTIONS

Try these other questions

H '03 I A6
H '02 I A12
H ' 99 I A13

H '04 I B4
H '03 I B5(b)
H '01 I B2
H '06 I B5(a)

Your revision notes

●●●**Learning Objectives**

Learn how to:

● apply an inflation rate to prices

Understand:

● what is meant by economics
● factors of production
● national income
● economic growth
● Ireland's resources

Tip

Tick each one off when you feel confident that you know it.

 **Understand**

Economics

Economics is the study of scarce resources and how best to use them to supply the goods and services that people need and want.

Needs and Wants

A need is something which is required to live. Food, clothing, shelter and clean water are all needs. Needs are limited.

Anything else is a want. Wants are unlimited.

Resources

All resources are scarce. That is, there are less of them than is needed to satisfy *all* needs and wants.

Choice

Because resources are scarce, choices have to be made about how they will be used.

Market

A place where goods or services are bought and sold.

Factors of Production

Resources are known as Factors of Production. To produce any good or supply any service all of the factors must be used.

Each factor receives an income.

Factors of production	Definition	Payment
Land	All natural resources (plants, animals, fish) as well as minerals from under the ground.	**Rent** is paid to use land.
Labour	Work done by people.	**Wages** are paid for work.
Capital	Goods used to produce other goods, e.g. machinery, buildings, roads etc. Buying them is called investment.	**Interest** is paid to investors to use their money.
Enterprise	The imagination to combine the other factors to form a business. Risk taking. The person is an **entrepreneur.**	Any money left after paying the other factors goes to the entrepreneur as **Profit.**

Ireland's Resources

Land Good agricultural land Lead and zinc Turf Gas A mild climate favourable for growing most crops	**Labour** An educated, young workforce from Ireland and abroad.
	Enterprise Ireland has many outstanding entrepreneurs: Tony O'Reilly (Newspapers, Crystal)
Capital A lot of money has been invested in Ireland's factories and infrastructure (roads, phone networks, etc.)	Martin Naughton (Heaters) Dermot Desmond (Finance) Tony Ryan (Aircraft) Michael Smurfit (Paper & Packaging).

The National Economy

In order to make the best use of these resources, different countries use different methods of making decisions.

Free Enterprise Also called a Free Market. Most choices are made by private individuals for their own benefit. e.g. USA.

Centrally Planned Economy The government decides what is produced and who will do it. They often decide on the price as well. e.g. China.

Mixed Economy Some decisions are made by the government; other decisions are made by private individuals. e.g. Ireland.

Measuring the Economy (Economic Indicators)

National Income

The total amount of goods and services produced in a country in one year, sometimes called Gross National Product (GNP).

Economic Growth

When GNP increases from one year to the next.

What happens with **high economic growth?**

> More jobs become available.
> Wages may increase.
> This may cause prices to increase.
> The government may receive more money in taxes.

What happens with **low economic growth?**

> If economic growth is less than population growth, unemployment will increase.

Unemployment

The percentage of people looking for employment but who are unable to find a job. What happens with **unemployment?**

> An unemployed person may have difficulty paying for day-to-day needs.
> Social welfare payments are a drain on government finance.
> Government tax revenue falls as unemployment increases.

National Debt

The total amount of money owed by the government. What happens with the **National Debt?**

> The opportunity cost of paying the debt is other things the goverment could do with the money.

79

Inflation

A persistent increase in the general level of prices.

What causes **Inflation?**

As their incomes increase, people have more money to spend.
If wages increase, employers may increase prices to recover the extra cost.
The price of important imported goods may increase (e.g. oil).

What happens with **inflation?**

As prices go up, money loses value.
If inflation was 11%, what could be bought for €100 last year would cost €111 this year.
In the same way, savings lose value.
The value of money borrowed also falls. This means that it becomes easier to repay a debt.
If inflation is higher in Ireland than in other countries, the price of goods made here will increase faster. They will become less competitive and exports may fall causing unemployment.

Interest Rates

Interest is the price of capital (money). The rate is set by the European Central Bank.
What happens with **high interest rates?**

Entrepreneurs will be unwilling to invest. As a result, no new jobs will be created.
Higher interest rates mean higher mortgage repayments. People have less money to spend on other things, e.g. new car, holiday.

What happens with **low interest rates?**

Companies are more willing to invest creating employment.

How to

Calculations with Inflation

1 Calculate the price

Sample Question

H '00 I B3(d)

A family's weekly grocery bill costs €111 in January 1999. If the inflation rate for the year was 11%, what would the same groceries have cost in January, 2000?

Answer

Price in 1999	€111
Increase in prices	€111 × 11% = + €12.21
Price in 2000 =	€123.21

2 Calculate the rate of inflation

Sample Question

H '03 I A20

Year 1   Cost of Living =   €20,000
Year 2   Cost of Living =   €21,500
Calculate the rate of inflation to one decimal point.

Answer

$$\frac{(€21,500 - €20,000)}{€20,000} \times 100 = 7.5\%$$

Question

Try these other questions

O '03 A4

Fill in the missing factors of production in the spaces provided.

	Labour		Enterprise

O'01A10

Column 1 is a list of terms. Column 2 is a list of possible explanations for these terms.

Match the two lists by placing the letter of the correct explanation beside the relevant number below. (Note that one explanation does not refer to any of the terms.)

letter	Column 1	Column 2
	1. Opportunity Cost	A. When something is in short supply
	2. Scarcity	B. Having to sacrifice one item to buy another
	3. Inflation	C. A tax on buying goods
		D. A rise in the general price of goods

O'99A12

To a teenager in Ireland, which of the following are NEEDS and which are WANTS? (Place a tick (✓) in the appropriate box in each case.

	NEEDS	WANTS
a) Clothes		
b) Computer Games		
c) Food		

H'02 1 B6

Ireland has achieved very high levels of economic growth in the past ten years.
i)   What is meant by the term economic growth?   (3)
iii) Name TWO economic consequences resulting from this growth in the economy.   (7)

H '00 1 B3

What is meant by the term inflation?

Give one cause of inflation.

The present rate of inflation in Ireland is nearest to which one of the following figures?

2%

10%

18%

27%

(12)

Questions

H '04 I B3(d)

H '02 I B6(d)

H '06 I A17

H '06 I B3(a)

●●●**Learning Objectives**

Learn how to:

- use given figures to prepare a national budget

Understand:

- services provided by government
  (capital/current expenditure)
- sources of government income
  (capital/current income)

Tip

Tick each one off when
you feel confident that
you know it.

REVISE WISE
TIP

Understand

REVISE WISE
UNDERSTANDING

National Budget
. . . .

The planned income and expenditure of the Government.
The work of the government is divided into **departments**, each providing
different services.

Current Expenditure
Day-to-day expenditure by the government.

Capital Expenditure

Expenditure on things which will last more than a year,
e.g.

Department	Current expenditure	Capital expenditure
Department of Health and Children	Medical cards, nurses' and doctors' pay	Building hospitals, clinics, purchasing hospital equipment
Department of Education and Science	Teachers' pay, school running costs	School buildings and equipment
Department of Justice, Equality and Law Reform	Garda pay, Judges' pay	Building prisons, court buildings
Department of the Environment	Commercial vehicle testing	Building waste treatment facilities

Current Income (Revenue)

Money the government receives on a regular basis.
- *Income Tax:* Tax deducted from the income of workers.
- *Value Added Tax:* Tax on the value of goods bought.
- *Corporation Tax:* Tax on the profits earned by companies.
- *Customs Duty:* Tax on imports of some goods.
- *Excise:* Tax on certain goods (e.g. tobacco, petrol, alcohol) wherever they are produced.
- *Other:* Plastic bag levy, dividend from semi-state companies, Stamp Duty.

Capital Income (Revenue)

Once-off income the government receives from various sources.
- *Privatising:* Selling state owned companies (e.g. Aer Lingus).
- *Transfers:* Money received from the European Union (road building, sewerage treatment, etc.).
- *Borrowing:* Required to finance expenditure over and above government income.

Government Budget

Balanced Budget: Current income is equal to current expenditure.
Budget Surplus: Current income is greater than current expenditure.
Budget Deficit: Current income is less than current expenditure.

What to do with a surplus?

- pay for capital expenditure
- it can be used to pay part of the National Debt

What to do about a deficit?

- increase tax rates or introduce new taxes (e.g. a tax on milk cartons)
- reduce expenditure
- use other sources of finance (privatisation, selling oil exploration licences)

Local Government

- provides local services such as parks, water, sewerage, public libraries, and housing
- financed by:
  - ○ charging for the services it provides
  - ○ levying rates (a tax based on the value of the property) on commercial occupiers (shops, factories etc.)
  - ○ receives a large proportion of its income from the central exchequer

 **How to**

Prepare a National Budget

Sample Question

The following figures were produced by the Minister for Finance on Budget day as projections for the year 2007. From the information given, draft the National Budget and say if it is a Surplus or Deficit Budget.

Main items of revenue and Expenditure	Estimated figures in millions €
Agriculture	137
Corporation Tax	77
Customs Duty	24
Debt Servicing	237
Defence	86
DIRT	139
Education & Science	330
Excise Duty	148
Health & Social Welfare	509
PAYE	619
VAT	170

Answer

Solution

Current Budget	
Expenditure	**€(million)**
Health & Social Welfare	509
Education & Science	330
Defence	86
Debt Servicing	237
Agriculture	137
Total Expenditure	**1,299**
PAYE	619
Customs Duty	24
DIRT	139
Excise Duty	148
VAT	170
Corporation Tax	77
Total Income	**1,177**
Surplus (Current Account)	**122**

Questions

Try these other questions

O '98 B7 (excerpt)

In a country called Softland, the following figures were published by the government for the year 1997.

i)   Using all of the figures below, prepare the Softland government's budget for the year 1997. (15)

ii) State whether it is a surplus or a deficit budget. (5)

Current Budget	
	€(million)
Expenditure	
Health	3,000
Education	1,500
Social Welfare	4,000
Agriculture	1,000
Debt Servicing	2,000
Other	3,500
Income	
Income tax	4,750
Customs & Excise	3,250
VAT	5,500
Other	2,750

O '03 A10

Match the budget types in Column 1 with the explanations in Column 2 by placing the letter of the correct explanation under the relevant number below.

Letter	Budget Type	Explanation
	1. Balanced Budget	a. Income is greater than expenditure
	2. Budget Surplus	b. Income is less than expenditure
	3. Budget Deficit	c. Income equals expenditure

O '03 A11

Customs duty is a tax on:

Imports	☐
Exports	☐
Employment	☐

(Tick (✓) the most suitable box)

Questions

Try these other questions

H '04 I B3 (a,b,c)

H '02 I B6 (a,b,c)

H '01 I B4

Your revision notes

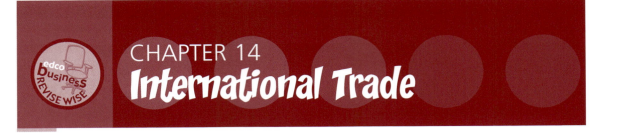

CHAPTER 14
International Trade

Learn how to:

- prepare Balance of Trade accounts
- prepare Balance of Payments accounts
- prepare foreign exchange calculations
- identify surplus versus deficit

Understand:

- Ireland's principal imports/exports
- Ireland's principal trading partners
- countries of the EU, languages, currencies
- Eurozone countries
- currencies of other trading partners (e.g. USA, Japan)
- import substitution

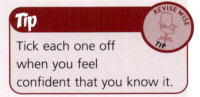

Tip

Tick each one off when you feel confident that you know it.

Understand

Trading

Importing: Buying goods/services from abroad.
Imports can be visible or invisible
Visible imports: Goods which can be seen coming into the country.
Invisible imports: Mostly services. Nothing can be seen coming into the country, but the money going out can be measured.

Exporting: Selling goods and services abroad.
Exports can also be visible or invisible.

Ireland's Principal Imports and Exports

	Visible	Invisible
Imports	Oil products (petrol, diesel) Cars Electronic goods (TV, mobile phone, stereo) Domestic appliances (fridge, cooker) Machinery	An Irish person flying with British Airways Income earned by foreign rock bands performing here Money spent by Irish people when on holiday abroad (hotels, food, etc.)
Exports	Computers and computer parts (Intel, Dell) Meat (beef, chicken, pork) Dairy Products Pharmaceuticals	Money spent by non-residents on holiday here Money earned by Ryanair for flying non-residents into Ireland and between overseas airports Money earned by banks, insurance companies etc. providing services to non-residents

Ireland's Principal Trading Partners

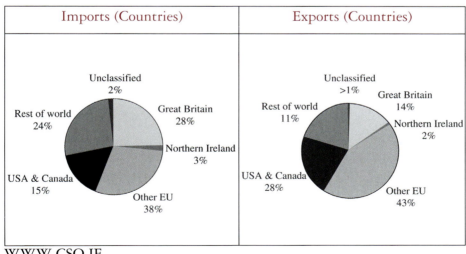

Imports (Countries)	Exports (Countries)
Unclassified 2%	Unclassified >1%
Great Britain 28%	Great Britain 14%
Northern Ireland 3%	Northern Ireland 2%
Other EU 38%	Other EU 43%
USA & Canada 15%	USA & Canada 28%
Rest of world 24%	Rest of world 11%

WWW.CSO.IE

Reasons for International Trade

1 Shortage of certain resources that are needed (oil being the main one)
2 Climate not suitable for certain products (e.g. oranges, rice, cotton)
3 To produce exports (computer parts, raw materials for the pharmaceutical industry)
4 Irish firms export to make more profit
5 To pay for imports

 **How to**

Balance of Payments

The difference between the total flow of money coming into Ireland and the total flow going out. It is made up of two parts.

Balance of Trade
Shows the balance between visible exports and imports.

Balance of Invisible Trade
The balance between invisible imports and exports.

Import Substitution

Making goods in Ireland which used to be imported or buying Irish-made goods instead of importing them.

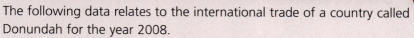

Sample Question

The following data relates to the international trade of a country called Donundah for the year 2008.

	€
Visible Exports	13 billion
Invisible Exports	21.3 billion
Visible Imports	17.2 billion
Invisible Imports	9.7 billion

Calculate the following trade figures in relation to Donundah and state whether they are a surplus or a deficit.
Show your workings.
- i) Balance of Trade
- ii) Balance of Payments

Solution

i) Balance of Trade:

Visible Exports	13.0 billion
Visible Imports	17.2 billion
Balance	4.2 billion (deficit)

ii) Balance of Payments

Balance of Trade:

Visible Exports	13 billion
Visible Imports	17.2 billion
Balance	4.2 billion (deficit)

Invisible Trade:

Invisible Exports	21.3 billion
Invisible Imports	9.7 billion
Balance	11.6 billion (surplus)
Balance of Payments	7.4 billion (surplus)

Understand

The EU

- a free-trade area with no restrictions on the movement of goods, capital or labour. It has grown from the original six countries to twenty-five countries and a number of other countries have applied to join
- twelve countries in the EU adopted a single currency in 2001 (the Euro)

Advantages of the single currency (Euro):

1. Businesses importing and exporting don't have the expense of changing currencies in the bank
2. Exchange rates rise and fall. A business is never certain how much an import will cost or how much an export will sell for unless there is a single currency
3. It is easier to compare prices on holiday or when buying online

Member States of the European Union

Country	Capital	Language	Currency
Austria	Vienna	German	Euro
*Belgium	Brussels	Dutch, French, German	Euro
Cyprus	Nicosia	Greek/ Turkish	Cypriot Pound
Czech Republic	Prague	Czech	Koruna
Denmark	Copenhagen	Danish	Krone
Estonia	Tallinn	Estonian	Kroon
Finland	Helsinki	Finnish/ Swedish	Euro
*France	Paris	French	Euro
*Germany	Berlin	German	Euro
Greece	Athens	Greek	Euro
Hungary	Budapest	Hungarian	Forint
Ireland	Dublin	Gaeilge/ English	Euro
*Italy	Rome	Italian	Euro
Latvia	Riga	Latvian	Lat

Member States of the European Union (continued)

Country	Capital	Language	Currency
Lithuania	Vilnius	Lithuanian	Lit
*Luxembourg	Luxembourg	Luxembourgian/ French/ German	Euro
Malta	Valletta	Maltese/ English	Lira
*Netherlands	The Hague	Dutch	Euro
Poland	Warsaw	Polish	Zloty
Portugal	Lisbon	Portuguese	Euro
Slovakia	Bratislava	Slovak	Koruna
Slovenia	Ljubljana	Slovene	Tolar
Spain	Madrid	Spanish	Euro
Sweden	Stockholm	Swedish	Krona
United Kingdom	London	English	Pound (Sterling)

* The original member states

Other major trading partners

Country	Capital	Currency
China	Beijing	Yuan
Japan	Tokyo	Yen
United States of America	Washington D.C.	(US) Dollar
Canada	Ottawa	(Canadian) Dollar

How to

Foreign Exchange Calculation

The rate of exchange is the value of one currency against another.

To convert Euro to another currency, *multiply* by the '**Bank Sells**' exchange rate.

To convert a currency back to Euro, *divide* by the '**Bank Buys**' exchange rate.

Sample Questions

1. A UK importer is paid STG£12,400 for a new machine from an Irish supplier. Your local bank had the following information on a display board in the bank:

	Bank Sells	Bank Buys
Sterling	0.6171	0.6234

Calculate the cost of the machine in Euro

Solution

You want to sell Sterling, so the bank is buying Sterling.
£12,400 / 0.6234 ≈ €19890.92

2. If the rate of exchange is €1 = US$1.20, how much would you receive if you converted €2,468 to dollars?

Solution

You want to buy dollars, so the bank is selling them.
2,468 x 1.20 ≈ 2961.6

Questions

Try these other questions

H '04 I A5   H '03 I B4
H '02 I A 8   H '98 I B5(b)
H '01 I A3
H '01 I A15
H '06 I B3(c)

●●● Learning Objectives

Learn how to:

- compare businesses under the headings: control, finance, profits, ownership, size

Understand:

- limited liability, shareholders, privatisation, Annual General Meeting
- sole trader, private limited company (Ltd), co-operative, state ownership
- state companies and what they do

Tip

Tick each one off when you feel confident that you know it.

Understand

Definitions

Shareholder: One of the owners of a company.

Annual General Meeting (AGM): The main meeting of the shareholders and directors of a company.

Limited Liability: If a business fails, the shareholders' responsibility is limited to the amount of money they have invested already, i.e. they can only lose the amount of money they have invested.

Privatisation: If a state-owned company is sold into private ownership. Several former semi-state companies have been privatised in recent years

Was Semi-State	*Now*
Telecom Éireann	Eircom plc.
Irish Sugar	Greencore plc.
Irish Life Assurance Corporation	(part of) Irish Life and Permanent plc

The owners of a company can organise themselves in different ways.

Sole Trader

An individual goes into business for him/herself, e.g., hairdresser, family doctor (GP).

Advantages

1 Very easy to set up
2 Decisions can be made quickly
3 The owner gets to keep all the profit

Disadvantages

1 Unlimited liability
2 Difficult to raise money to expand the business
3 The owner has to do everything

Co-operative

Seven or more people get together to form a co-operative. Most co-ops in Ireland are either agricultural *producer* co-ops (e.g. Mitchelstown Co-op) or *financial* co-ops (e.g. local credit union).
Shareholders in a co-op are called members.

Advantages

1 Limited liability
2 One person cannot buy control of the co-op by buying more shares
3 Profits are shared among members as a dividend per share

Disadvantages

1 As all members get one vote, some may be reluctant to invest more money
2 May not have the professional management skills and experience required

Private Limited Company (Ltd or Teo after the name)

One or more people get together to go into business. The company is run by a board of directors on behalf of the shareholders. Shareholders may also be directors.

Advantages

1 Easier to raise finance
2 Limited liability
3 If a shareholder dies, the business continues

Disadvantages

1 Laws and regulations about setting up and running a limited company
2 A shareholder may have difficulty selling their shares

State ownership

The government owns a number of companies that provide certain goods and services to industry and to consumers.
The main reasons for this are:
1 Private enterprise was unable/unwilling to spend that much money to set up the company (ESB)

2 To provide essential services at a minimum price (Bus Éireann, Iarnród Éireann)

3 To exploit Ireland's natural resources (Bord na Móna, Coillte, Dublin Docklands Authority)

4 To provide certain non-commercial services (Fáilte Ireland, Industrial Development Authority)

State owned companies

Name	Main Activity
Aer Rianta	Airport management
Bord na Móna	Exploiting Irish peatlands (fuel, and peat moss for gardening)
Bord Iascaigh Mhara (BIM)	Encouraging the Irish Sea fishing industry by providing marketing and training.
Bord Bia	Promotion of Irish-produced food at home and abroad
Coillte	Planting, managing and harvesting Irish forests. Producing and marketing timber products and Christmas trees
Córas Iompar Éireann (CIE) (operating as three companies) Bus Éireann Dublin Bus Iarnród Éireann (Irish Rail)	Public transport services National bus service Buses in Dublin National rail network
Electricity Supply Board (ESB)	Generating and distributing electricity
Enterprise Ireland	Supports the development of native companies
Industrial Development Authority (IDA)	Supports foreign companies setting up in Ireland
Foras Áiseanna Saothair (FÁS)	Training of the unemployed, apprentices and workers
Met Éireann	Weather forecasting
An Post	National postal service
Radio Telefís Éireann (RTÉ)	Radio and television programmes
Voluntary Health Insurance	Insurance to pay for hospital expenses

 **How to**

The different forms of ownership can be compared under different headings.

	Sole Trader	Private Limited Company (Ltd/Teo)	Co-operative	State Ownership
Ownership	The owner is the business	1–50 shareholders	More than 7 shareholders	The company is owned by the government
Liability	Unlimited	Limited	Limited	Limited
Control	Owner has total control	Each shareholder gets one vote for each share owned	Each shareholder gets one vote. (no matter how many shares owned)	The government has full control
Finance	The owner invests their own money	To raise more money, more shares can be sold to new or existing shareholders	To raise more money, more shares can be sold to new or existing shareholders	The government may invest more capital. (Under EU competition law they may be prevented from doing this.)
Profits	All profits go to the owner as income	tProfits may be retained by the company or returned to the shareholders as a DIVIDEND	Profits may be retained by the co-operative or returned to the shareholders as a DIVIDEND	Profits may be retained by the company or returned to the State as a DIVIDEND. Some state-owned companies are not intended to make a profit
Size	Usually small	Usually small to medium size	Some of the biggest companies in Ireland are co-ops. Most are small to medium	State-owned companies tend to be quite large

Questions

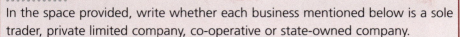

Try these other questions

O '02 B7

In the space provided, write whether each business mentioned below is a sole trader, private limited company, co-operative or state-owned company.

	The businesses are	
1	Bord na Móna	
2	John Lyons, Butcher	
3	Credit Union	
4	Ceol Wholesalers Ltd	
5	RTÉ	

O '99 A7

Tick (✓) the most appropriate answer below:

A Private Limited Company is

A business owned by one person	☐
A business owned by the state	☐
A business owned by between one and fifty people	☐

H '02 II (3)

Explain **two** of the following forms of ownership:

   i) Sole Trader, ii) Co-operative, iii) State Ownership

H '02 I A10

Name a state-owned company/body involved in the following activities:

1 Promoting exports _____

2 Communications _____

H '02 I A11

Tick (✓) the correct box to show whether the following statements are true or false

		True	False
(a)	In a co-operative, shareholders have limited liability	☐	☐
(b)	In a co-operative, each shareholder has only one vote	☐	☐

H '98 II (2)

Explain two advantages of forming a Private Limited Company.

CHAPTER 16
Services for Business

●●●**Learning Objectives**

Learn how to:

- prepare cash flow statement
- assess creditworthiness
- operate a business account
- prepare a business plan
- calculate an insurance premium

Understand:

- safe deposit, night safe
- credit rating
- government grants, factoring, retained profits
- fidelity guarantee, product liability, public liability, employer's PRSI, export credit

Tip

Tick each one off when you feel confident that you know it.

Understand

Financial Services for Business

The material in Chapters 9–11 is also relevant here. This chapter deals with additional material that relates to business banking only.

Commercial Banks

In addition to the services mentioned in Chapter 9, students should understand:

- electronic Fund Transfer at Point Of Sale (laser machine at the till)
- credit card services (payment and collection)
- credit check/credit rating for customers
- night safe (a drawer on the bank wall where money can be deposited at night)

Merchant Banks

Merchant banks are smaller banks that provide a more personal service for businesses. They also provide services not readily available from the commercial banks:

- share dealing
- export credit insurance
- debt collection services

Operating a Business Bank Account

To open a bank account, a private limited company will need the following:

- name and address of business
- certificate of incorporation
- signatures of people who can write company cheques
- written agreement of directors to open the current account
- a business will need at least **two signatures** to operate a cheque book and to make any withdrawals from the bank

Financial Planning For Business

Any business needs to plan for the future.

They need to identify what they need money for, how much they need and when they will need it.

Sources of Finance

In addition to those mentioned in chapter 10:

Short term	Less than 1 year
Trade Credit	Goods are not paid for immediately. Paying 30 days later is common
Accrued Expenses	Delaying the payment of the ESB or phone bill means that the money is available for other purposes
Taxation	Money collected as VAT is paid to the Revenue Commissioners every 2 months Money collected as PAYE and PRSI is paid up to a month after it is deducted
Factoring	The sum owed by a debtor is sold to a third party for immediate cash
Used to pay for stock and the day-to-day expenses of the business	

Medium term	1 to 5 years
Term Loan	Given for a specific purpose and repaid in regular instalments
Leasing	Renting for a fixed term. Regular payments made, but the firm will never own the asset

Used to buy machinery, motor vehicles etc.	
Grants	Money from the EU or the government to help the business expand. Grants do not have to be repaid
Business Expansion Scheme	A scheme to encourage people to invest in business. The investment can be used to reduce the investors' income tax bill
Sale and Leaseback	An asset is sold for cash and then leased back
Used to pay for longer term investments, e.g. buildings	

Long term	Over 5 years
Capital	Money invested by the owners or new investors
Mortgage	A loan secured on property
Debenture	A fixed interest long-term loan taken out by a business
Retained Earnings	Profits made by the company are not paid as dividends, but reinvested in the business

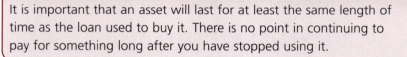

Tip

It is important that an asset will last for at least the same length of time as the loan used to buy it. There is no point in continuing to pay for something long after you have stopped using it.

Borrowing

If the **business** decides to borrow, it should answer the following questions:

1 Why? (Purpose of the loan)
2 How Much? (Amount to borrow)
3 How Long? (Period of the loan)
4 Cost? (The *interest rate* and *monthly payments*)
5 Collateral? (What security can it offer?)

The **lender** will want to know if the business will be able to make the repayments. It will get this information by examining:

1 Business plan
2 Cash flow statement
3 Financial accounts
4 Collateral offered

How to

Applying for a Loan

How to complete an *Application Form* is explained in chapter 10.
You may be asked to write a letter of application for a loan.
The layout of the *Letter* is as given in Chapter 7, but the letter must contain the following points:

1 How much do you want?
2 What do you want it for?
3 Why do you need to borrow?
4 When will you repay?
5 What evidence can you give to support your application?

This might include a Cash Flow Forecast, a Business Plan and a copy of your Profit and Loss account (see chapter 34) for the past few years.

Cash Flow Forecast/Statement

A household prepares a budget in order to plan for future income and expenditure. A Cash Flow Forecast is the same thing for a business and the layout is very similar.
A business may prepare a Cash Flow Statement in order to:

● compare expected future revenue and expenditure of an investment to see if it is worthwhile
● as evidence for a bank that the company will be able to meet the repayments on a loan

A Cash Flow Statement is similar to the Forecast but, instead of *predicting the future*, it *shows what really happened*.

Sample Question

Complete the partially completed Cash Flow Forecast form for St Paul's Ink Ltd for the months of September, October, November and December, as well as the total columns.
The following information should be taken into account:

● monthly sales are expected to increase by 20%, beginning in November
● the shareholders expect to borrow €45,000 in September
● an EU Grant of €20,000 is expected in November
● monthly purchases are expected to increase by 30% beginning in October
● wages and transport costs are expected to remain the same every month
● light and heat expenses are expected to increase by 25% in the months of September and November
● new buildings are expected to be purchased in September for €50,000
● shareholders are expected to be paid a dividend of €8,500 in December

Answer

Cash Flow Forecast for St Paul's Ink Ltd for the period Jan to June 2007

	July €	August €	September €	October €	November €	December €	Total Jul–Dec €
Receipts							-
Sales	15,000	15,000	15,000	15,000	18,000	18,000	96,000
Share Capital	50,000	45,000					95,000
Loan			45,000				45,000
EU Grant					20,000		20,000
A-Total Receipts	65,000	60,000	60,000	15,000	38,000	18,000	256,000
Payments							-
Purchases	4,500	4,500	4,500	5,850	5,850	5,850	31,050
Wages	7,000	7,000	7,000	7,000	7,000	7,000	42,000
Transport Costs	2,100	2,100	2,100	2,100	2,100	2,100	12,600
Light and Heat	3,600	-	4,500		4,500		12,600
Delivery Van		42,000					42,000
Buildings			50,000				42,000
Dividend						8,500	8,500
B-Total Payments	17,200	55,600	68,100	14,950	19,450	23,450	198,750
C-Net Cash (A-B)	47,800	4,400	-8,100	50	18,550	-5,450	57,250
D Opening Cash	2,500	50,300	54,700	46,600	46,650	65,200	2,500
Closing Cash	50,300	54,700	46,600	46,650	65,200	59,750	59,750

Business Plan

A way of setting out what the company is, what they hope to do and how they hope to do it. Different headings can be used, but the ones shown on page 108 are common.

Sample Question

Caoimhe McCooey and Stephen McGee decide to set up an ink supplies company to manufacture, distribute and sell refill inks for whiteboard markers.

The name of their company is St Paul's Ink Ltd, located at 123 Shy Bill Hill, Arklow, County Wicklow. Caoimhe McCooey is to be the Managing Director.

Their market research provides the following information:

- There are 20,000 potential customers
- There is only one competitor, but their product cannot be used to refill all brands of pen
- They estimate they can sell 50,000 units per year at €10 each.

They estimate their costs as follows: lease of premises €62,000; machinery €58,000; delivery van €15,000; working capital €25,000.

They have savings of €95,000.

1 Calculate the amount of they would need to borrow in order to set up this business.

2 Complete the blank Business Plan Document supplied, using today's date.

Your revision notes

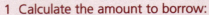

Answer

Solutions

1 Calculate the amount to borrow:

	Lease	62,000
+	*Machinery*	58,000
+	*Delivery Van*	15,000
+	*Working Capital*	25,000
	Total required	160,000
	Finance available	95,000
	160,000 – 95,000 =	65,000
	Amount to Borrow	65,000

2 Complete the Business Plan

Company Details

Name of Company	*St Paul's Ink Ltd*
Address of Company	*123 Shy Bill Hill,*
	Arklow,
	County Wicklow.
Shareholders/Owners	
	Caoimhe McCooey
	Stephen McGee
Managing Director	*Caoimhe McCooey*

Product

Description of product	*A low odour, non-toxic refill ink for whiteboard markers available in a range of colours. The refill pump means you don't need to open the pen.*

Market Research

Size of market	*20,000 units per year*
Competitors	*1 competitor (none with pump)*
Price per unit	*e10 including pump*

Sales Promotion Methods

Sample sent to schools, colleges. Advertising in trade magazines and point-of-sale displays in business stationers.

Finance

Total Required	*€ 160,000*
Amount Available	*€ 95,000*
Loan Required	*€ 65,000*
Signed	
	Caoimhe McCooey
	Stephen McGee
Date	*12-04-08*

Company Details

This section identifies the company, i.e. who owns it and who runs it.
A business plan may include the experience of the managers, especially if it is a new business setting up.

Product

What is the product and why it is better than anything else on the market?

Market Research

How many units do you expect to sell per day/week/month?
Who are your competitors?
The selling price you hope to get.
Advertising, leaflets, free samples, coupons, channels of distribution, etc.

Finance

How much will it cost? This should include the cost of setting up and running.
How much do you have already (i.e. capital invested by the owner)?
How much do you need to borrow?

Insurance For Business

A business needs to have insurance because:
1 it protects the business from *potential financial loss*
2 it is *legally required* to have certain insurance
   a. Motor insurance (for any vehicles owned)
   b. Employer's PRSI must be paid for each employee

Types of Insurance

As mentioned in chapter 11, insurance provides compensation if there is a loss due to a risk happening.
Bad management, bankruptcy and stock becoming obsolete are *uninsurable* risks.

Insurable Risks

- **Employer's Liability:** if an employee is injured in the course of their work
- **Public Liability:** for members of the public who are injured on the company's premises
- **Product Liability:** for anyone injured due to a defect in the product
- **Fire:** if the business is damaged due to a fire (either stock or premises)
- **Theft and Burglary**
- **Goods in Transit:** Damage to goods while being transported.
- **Cash in Transit:** Loss or theft of cash being transported (e.g. to the bank).
- **Bad Debt:** If a debtor is unable to pay the debt due to bankruptcy.
- **Fidelity Guarantee:** If an employee steals from the company.

- **Key person:** If someone important to the business becomes unable to work through death or illness.
- **Consequential Loss:** If the business loses money as a result of, for example, a strike in another company.
- **Export Credit:** If a foreign company fails to pay for goods.

Sample Question

Calculating a premium

Manannán Ltd requested an insurance quotation from Eblana Insurers Ltd for the following assets:

Buildings €320,000, Machinery €120,000, 5 Delivery vans at €34,000 each, Stock €25,000 and cash in office of €4,500.

Eblana insurers supplied the following quotation of one year's insurance.

Buildings and Machinery: €7 per €1,000 value
Delivery van: comprehensive cover €2,340 per van
Stock insurance: €22 per €1,000 value
Cash insurance: €20 per €500
New Business offer of 12% off total premium.

Manannán Ltd accepted the quotation and took out insurance on everything at replacement value except Buildings which they insured for €240,000. The premium was paid by cheque on 1 July 2008.

a) Calculate the total premium paid. (Show your workings clearly)

Answer

Solution

Item	Value €	Cost per unit	Units	Total €
Buildings	240,000	7	240	1,680
Machinery	120,000	7	120	840
Delivery Van	34,000	2,340	5	11,700
Stock	25,000	22	25	550
Cash in office	4,500	20	9	180
Total premium before discount				14,950
Discount (12%)				1,794
Premium to pay				13,156

Questions

Try these other questions

H '99 I A13

Name the type of insurance which a shop owner would take out to cover the following risks;

a) An employee being injured at work

_____

b) An employee stealing cash from the cash register

_____

H '98 I A16

Name two of the headings used in preparing a business plan

1. _____
2. _____

(from) H '95 I16

Nacsort Ltd Dundalk, manufacturers and retailers of household furniture for the Irish and European markets, seeks your advice regarding its insurance requirements.

Nascort has the following assets: Premises, Equipment, Motor Vans, Stock of Furniture.

It employs 60 workers and lodges its daily takings in a bank which is 20km away.

i) Give **two** types of insurance Nascort Ltd is required to have by law.

ii) Give **four other** types of insurance you would advise it to have.

iii) Explain the importance of having adequate insurance.

H '06 I A18

Outline two reasons why a company would prepare a business plan

(i) _____

(ii) _____

Questions

Business Plan	Cash Flow	Business Finance	Business insurance
H '04 II5(b (iii))	H '03 II6	H' 02 II4	H '00 II4 (a,b)
H '99 II5(b (iii))	H '98 II5 H '06 II 2(a)	H '00 II5(a,b(i,ii))	

CHAPTER 17
Communication

●●● **Learning Objectives**

Learn how to:

- identify a suitable medium for communication
- write a letter, memo, report

Understand:

- internal vs external communication
- visual, oral, written communication
- factors to consider in selecting a medium

Tip

Tick each one off when you feel confident that you know it.

 **Understand**

Communication: The transfer of a message from one person to another. The most effective communication is *Simple*, *Clear* and *Brief*.

Internal communication is communication from a person in a company to another person in the same company (managers, employees, supervisors, etc.).

External communication is between a person inside the company and someone outside the company (customers, suppliers, shareholders, the public).

Visual Communication	Oral Communication	Written Communication
Pictures	Meeting	Notice board
Graphs and Charts	Intercom	Fax
Posters	Telephone	e-mail
Films	Conference Call	Letter
Teletext	Video Conference	Memo
Website		Report
Notice Board		Text message
		Instant messaging (e.g. MSN)

Tip

Some forms of communication are a mix of two or more types and could be listed under either heading.

REVISE WISE
TIP

Some modern communication is directly from one computer to another. It is not intended for a human and so is not in a form a human can read, e.g. EDI (Electronic Data Interchange). EDI allows a computer in a shop to count how many units of a particular item have been sold (bar code scanner) and then *automatically* orders more of this item when the shop is about to run out.

Graphs and Charts

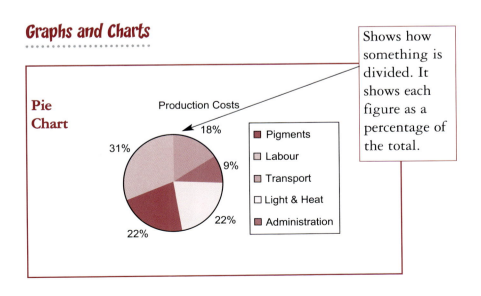

Pie Chart

Production Costs

Shows how something is divided. It shows each figure as a percentage of the total.

18%
9%
22%
22%
31%

- Pigments
- Labour
- Transport
- Light & Heat
- Administration

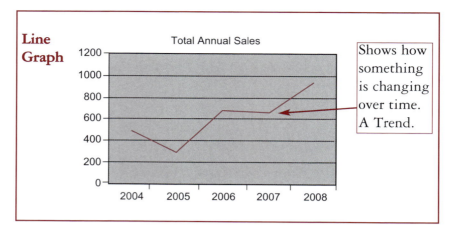

Line Graph — Shows how something is changing over time. A Trend.

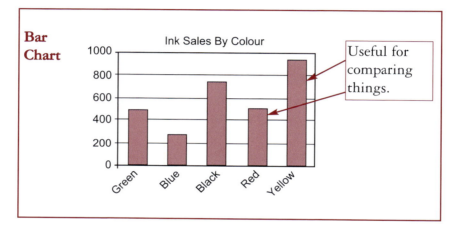

Bar Chart — Useful for comparing things.

If asked to show data on a graph or chart, ask yourself what are you showing and use the appropriate chart.

Tip

Be sure to include a title and to label everything clearly.

How to

Selecting a Medium of Communication

When selecting a medium of communication, consider the following factors:

1 Cost (How much?)
2 Speed (How long will it take?) Usually 'faster' will cost more, e.g. a letter in the post vs a courier?
3 Safety (Will the message get there at all?)
4 Confidentiality (Will people other than the intended recipient be able to read the message?)
5 Record (Is there a copy of the message as proof?)
6 Accuracy (Is the message received exactly the same as the message sent?)
7 Destination (Can the recipient receive the message? Do they have a fax-machine?)

Written Communication

Tip

In the exam you may be asked to write a letter, a memo or a report. It is important that you use the correct layout as marks will be lost if you do not.
The layout of a letter is given in Chapter 7.

Memo

A memo is a short message, handwritten or typed.
Most e-mail programmes use memo layout.

Sample Question

Draft a memo from Cormac Fitzpatrick, the secretary of the board of directors, to the directors, telling them that the meeting of 21-06-08 is being rescheduled for midday on 20-06-08, using today's date.

Solution

To: All Directors
From: The Secretary of the Board
Date: 12-06-08
Please note that the meeting scheduled for 21-06-08 is now to be held at 12 noon on 20-06-08
Signed: *Cormac Fitzpatrick*

Report

Sample Question

H'97 IB4

Na Fianna Sports Club, Clookeen, County Kerry, has one hundred members. It is considering the purchase of a new grass mower which has the retail price of €7,000. The club has got very little money to invest in it.

David Donnelly, the club's treasurer, approached Money Matters Ltd, Ballyvourney, County Cork, to investigate the sources and cost of a €7,000 loan to purchase the mower.

Ciara O'Mahony, Financial Consultant, working at Money Matters Ltd, investigated and came up with the following alternatives:

Option 1 Bank Loan. Borrow €7,000 for 3 years on which interest is charged at the flat rate of 11% per annum. The loan and interest would be repaid in six equal half yearly instalments.

Option 2 Hire Purchase. Pay a deposit of €500 plus 36 monthly instalments of €270 each.

Option 3 Rental Purchase. Pay a monthly rental of €190 each month for 4 years plus a final payment of €99 at the end of the lease to acquire ownership of the item.

On the 20 May 1997, the consultant wrote a report to the treasurer of the club, showing the total cost of each option and recommending the cheapest one. The consultant also suggested in the report that the club should organise some fund-raising activity. The money could be used to finance future capital.

Write the report which the consultant sent to the club's treasurer.

Answer

To: David Donnelly (Treasurer)
        Na Fianna Sports Club
        Clonkeen
        County Kerry

From: Ciara O'Mahony
        Financial Consultant

Terms of Reference:
        Investigate the sources and cost of a €7,000 loan to purchase a
        mower.

Findings
        In my investigation I found 3 options.
        1. Three year bank loan, with 6 half-yearly payments of €1,551.66.
           Total cost €9,310
        2. Hire purchase, with 36 monthly payments of €270, plus a deposit
           of €500. Total cost €10,220
        3. Rental Purchase, with 48 monthly payments of €190, plus a fixed
           payment of €99. Total cost of €9,219

Conclusions

Of those options, I recommend Rental Purchase. It has the cheapest total cost
and the lowest monthly repayments. However, I would suggest that the club
organise some fund-raising activities. The money raised could be used to pay
for future capital.

I am available to discuss any of the above

Signed

Ciara O'Mahony

Ciara O'Mahony
Financial Consultant
Money Matters Ltd
20 May 1997

Questions

Try these other questions

H '04 I A16

The following is a list of methods of communication. Which **two** of these are visual communications?

Tick (✓) the **two** correct answers only.

Letter	☐	Line graph	☐	Telephone	☐
Meeting	☐	Report	☐	Bar chart	☐

H '96 I A20

A sales agent for a product had total sales for the year of €240,000. The pie chart shows the breakdown of sales for the season. Show your workings.

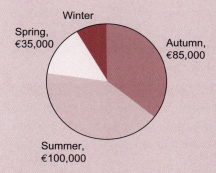

a) What percentage of total sales were in winter?

b) Name a product that might have a similar yearly sales cycle as the product sold by this agent.

H '96 II B4a

The following table shows the number of strikes in Ireland for the period 1990–1994.

Year	1990	1991	1992	1993	1994
Number of strikes	49	54	38	48	32

i) Illustrate the above information on a suitable chart or graph, using graph paper.

H '01 I A14

Indicate whether the following forms of communication are Visual, Written or Oral.

Tick (✓) the most suitable box in each case.

From	Oral	Written	Visual
Meeting			
Bar Charts			
Telephone			
Fax			

H '06 I A2

Tick (✓) whether the following forms of communication are INTERNAL or EXTERNAL

FORM OF COMMUNICATION	INTERNAL	EXTERNAL
Intercom		
Fax		
Notice Board		
Memorandum		

In the past there have been no questions entirely on communications. However, you may be asked to write a letter, report or memo as a part of a question on another topic

Questions

Letter	Report	Memo
H '03 I B6(a(I))	H '02 II 6(b)	H '01 I B6(b(ii))
H '99 I B4	H '00 II 5(b)	

●●●**Learning Objectives**

Learn how to:

- identify a suitable channel of distribution

Understand:

- primary, secondary, tertiary
- channels of distribution
- role and types of wholesaler
- functions and types of retailer

Tip

Tick each one off when you feel confident that you know it.

The Economy is Divided into Three Sectors

Sector	Definition	Examples
Primary	Extracting or using natural resources	Mining, agriculture, fishing (including fish farming), forestry
Secondary	Processing raw materials into manufactured goods	Construction, manufacturing
Tertiary	Doing something *with*, *to* or *for* someone	Banking, insurance, barber/hair dresser, restaurant, Gardaí

 ## How to

Channels of Distribution

The steps a good goes through to get from the producer/manufacturer to the consumer.

Traditional	Perishable	Direct sales	Mail order
Manufacturer	Manufacturer	Manufacturer	Manufacturer
↓	↓	↓	↓
Wholesaler	↓	↓	Wholesaler
↓	↓	↓	↓
Retailer	Retailer	↓	↓
↓	↓	↓	↓
Consumer	Consumer	Consumer	Consumer

Examples

Chocolate bar bought in local shop	Fresh vegetables	Clothes bought in a 'factory shop'	Books bought online from Amazon

Tip

Producers chose different channels of production depending on the type of product. Bulky goods with a long shelf life are usually distributed by traditional channels.

Goods with a short shelf life (daily newspapers, fresh milk) are often distributed to the retailer who then sells to the consumer.

 **Understand**

Wholesaler

A wholesaler is a business that buys from the producer and sells to retailers.

Traditional Wholesalers
- buy goods in bulk
- they may blend and/or package
- they usually sell on credit and deliver the goods.

Cash and Carry wholesalers
- buy in bulk
- do not blend or package
- sell to retailers in smaller quantities for cash
- Do not deliver

Wholesalers provide the following services:

Services to the producer	Services to the retailer
Buys in bulk	Sells in smaller quantities (Breaks Bulk)
Blends and packages	Delivers the goods
Stores the goods	Gives credit
Provides market information	Provides a range of goods from different manufacturers
Advertises and promotes the goods	

Different Types of Retailer

1 **Independent retailers:** Small business run by one person (a sole trader), e.g. a butcher, newsagents.
2 **Supermarkets:** Large self-service shops. Generally sell more cheaply, than independent shops.
3 **Chain stores:** A number of shops owned by the same company, e.g. supermarkets, sportswear (Champion Sports) or books (Eason's).
4 **Voluntary retail groups:** Shops that agree to buy their goods from a particular wholesaler and to trade under one name, e.g. Centra, Spar, Gala, etc.
5 **Convenience stores:** Small supermarkets that stay open late into the night.
6 **Discount stores:** Like supermarkets but by leaving the goods in the box, they save money. They have less staff and few shelves (e.g. Aldi, Lidl).
7 **Department stores:** A variety of types of goods sold in different parts of the store, e.g. Clerys, Shaw's.
8 **Shopping centres:** A variety of shops selling a range of goods located under one roof.

Recent developments in retailing

1 **Internet selling:** Goods are sold through a website. Goods may be delivered through the Internet (e.g. anti-virus software) or the goods may be delivered by post. A variation of this is selling games, ringtones etc. on mobile phones.
2 **Party selling:** An agent for a particular manufacturer organises a party at home, inviting friends and neighbours. They get to sample the goods and see them at work. Make-up (Avon) and kitchen equipment (Tupperware) is often sold this way.

Questions

Try these other questions

H' OO I A14

Study the following channel of distribution.

Manufacturer → Retailer → Consumer

a) Why would the wholesaler be omitted from a channel of distribution?

b) Give one service provided by the retailer for the consumer.

H '97 II 5

a) i) What is meant by the term channels of distribution?

   ii) Describe (illustrate) **three** channels of distribution and give an example of a good distributed by each channel.

O '98 B8

Jason mixed up the answers in his Business Studies test. He had all the correct answers but he put them in the wrong sentences.

Here is what he wrote:

Primary Production is *where teachers, nurses and hairdressers are employed.*

Secondary Production is *where raw materials are produced.*

The Service Industry is *where raw materials are turned into finished goods.*

The Wholesaler is *a shop that sells airline tickets.*

A Department Store is *a slot machine where you can buy cans of orange.*

A Shopping Centre is *a retailer with branches around the country.*

A Chain Store is *a shop that sells newspapers.*

A Vending Machine is *a covered area where there are many shops.*

A travel agency is *a person who buys in bulk (large amounts) from the Manufacturer.*

A newsagent is *one shop divided into many sections.*

a) Write out each sentence *fully* in your *Answer Book* showing the correct answer in each sentence.

b) Name two other types of retail shop that are not mentioned above, and state the service that each of them provides.

H '06 II 5 (a,b,c)

H '06 I A19

H '06 I A5

●●●Learning Objectives

Learn how to:

- draft an organisational structure

Understand:

- work vs employment
- unemployment, self-employment
- skilled, unskilled, semi-skilled, professional
- rights and responsibilities

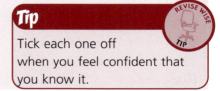

Tip

Tick each one off when you feel confident that you know it.

Understand

Definitions

Work is when a person does something productive. You work when you do homework, study or help at home.

Employment is when a person gets paid to work. If you have a job in a shop, you are **employed**.

Unemployment: If a person is looking for employment but cannot find a job, they are said to be unemployed.

To be counted as unemployed you must be between 16 and 66, available for work and not in full-time education. A person must be looking for work to be counted as unemployed.

The Labour Force: Made up of the total number of employed, unemployed and self-employed.

Types of Employees

Unskilled work is work which does not require any special training. It often involves physical labour and the rate of pay tends to be low, e.g. bin collector.

Semi-skilled work requires some training. Most semi-skilled workers are trained to use one machine or do one job, e.g. a person trained to use a sewing machine.

Skilled work requires specialist training to do a particular job. Carpenters and hairdressers are skilled.

Professional workers have a professional qualification, usually from a university. They need this qualification to do particular work, e.g. teachers, solicitors, doctors.

Natures of Work

The work done may be described as:

Manual involves physical work, such as gardening.

Clerical involves typing, filing, etc. (e.g. receptionist, bank teller).

Creative requires imagination, e.g. writer, artist, designer.

Administrative involves supervising or managing the work of others.

As an **employee**, you have certain rights and responsibilities:

Rights of the Employee	Responsibilities of the Employee
Fair day's pay	For a fair day's work
To be treated equally to other employees (pay, promotion etc.)	Abide by rules and regulations of workplace
Minimum number of paid holidays per year (legal minimum is 18 for full-time employees)	Not to give away company secrets or confidential information
To join a union if you want	Co-operate with other workers
To work in a healthy, safe environment	To look after your employer's property

Self-employment: If a person is working for themselves, they are in self-employment. Sole traders are self-employed.

Rewards of self-employment	Risks of self-employment
You are your own boss and can make your own decisions	If the business fails, you may lose your investment
Any profits are yours to keep	May have to work long hours
Working times to suit you and your customers	Have to provide the capital to set up and run the business
Decide what product or service to sell	Unlimited liability. You risk losing everything if your business fails

How to

Organisational Structure

In order to run a company it needs to be organised, that is, everybody has their own responsibilities and duties. Some people have a responsibility to oversee the work of others and they in turn are overseen by others.

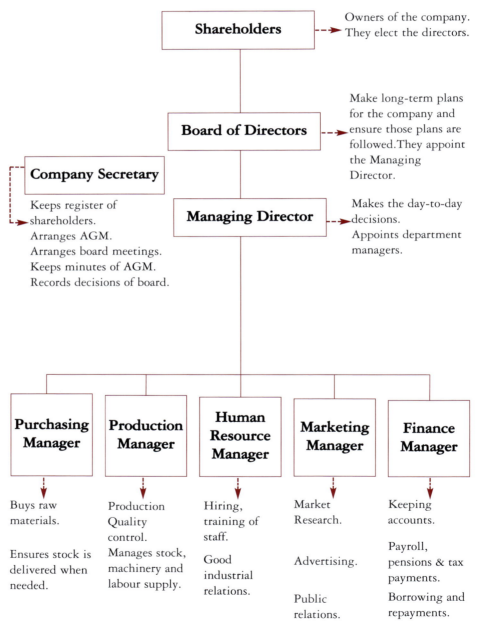

All department managers must also keep records for their departments

Sample Question

H '96 I A1

Complete the organisational chart below by writing in the appropriate terms in the blank spaces marked A and B.

Solution:

```
Shareholders
    ↓
Board of Directors
    ↓
Managing Director
    ↓
Department Managers
    ↓
Supervisors
    ↓
Staff Workers
```

Questions

Try the following questions

H '94 I A16

Place a tick (✓) opposite *each* statement to indicate whether it is true or false.

The *labour force* includes	True	False
a) Old-aged pensioners	☐	☐
b) University students	☐	☐
c) Unemployed people seeking employment	☐	☐
d) All employed People	☐	☐

H '04 I B6b (i, ii, iii)

H '95 I B5

H '02 I B 4c(ii)

Employers

●●● **Learning Objectives**

Learn how to:

- draft a job advertisement
- prepare a wages book

Understand:

- rights and responsibilities
- procedure for employing
- piece rate, time rate, commission, P45, P60

Tip

Tick each one off when you feel confident that you know it.

 **Understand**

Employers Also Have Certain Rights and Responsibilities

Rights of the employer	Responsibilities of the employer
To hire suitable staff	Equal pay for equal work
To expect employees to be loyal to the business	To give terms and conditions of employment in writing (a contract)
To decide the objectives of the business	To allow staff their annual paid holidays
To fire staff if there is a legitimate reason (e.g. stealing)	To keep appropriate records for tax purposes, etc.
	To maintain a safe and healthy workplace
	To ensure there is no discrimination in the workplace

The Procedure For Employing New Staff

1 **Job description** (what needs to be done?)
2 **Advertise** (newspapers, internet)
3 **Letter of application**, a CV, an application form from candidates
4 **Short listing** (the best candidates are picked out)
5 **Interview**
6 **Selection** (most suitable candidate)
7 **Candidate** is notified
8 **Contract** (terms and conditions of work, e.g. hours, pay, holidays, benefits in kind)
9 **Training** of the new employee
10 Employer and employee **inform local tax offices**. Arrangements are made to make the correct *PAYE and PRSI deductions*
11 **Probationary period** before being permanently employed

Job Advertisement

A job advertisement needs to:
1 Name the employer
2 Position to be filled
3 Qualifications and experience of the candidate
4 Personality of the candidate
5 How to apply
6 Closing date
7 State that the company is an equal opportunities employer

The advertisement may be placed in a newspaper, magazine, on radio or Teletext, on the Internet, or even in a shop window.

Tip

It is illegal for an employer to state a preference for one type of employee (e.g. 'young' or 'no immigrants').

Sample Job Advertisement from H '03 I B6

<table>
<tr><td colspan="2" align="center">SWIFT ELECTRONICS</td></tr>
<tr><td>Required:</td><td>Electronic Technician to join our maintenance team</td></tr>
<tr><td>Qualifications:</td><td>Electronic Engineering qualification
Two years' work experience</td></tr>
<tr><td>Candidate:</td><td>He/she should be hard-working, self-motivating, with good communication skills</td></tr>
<tr><td>Apply to:</td><td>Human Resource Manager
Swift Electronics
Fermoy
Co. Cork</td></tr>
<tr><td>Closing Date:</td><td>1st June 2003</td></tr>
<tr><td colspan="2" align="center">SWIFT ELECTRONICS is an equal opportunities employer</td></tr>
</table>

 **Understand**

Calculating Rates of Pay

1 **Time Rate:** you are paid a rate per hour for a normal working week (usually 39 hours). Extra work is paid with **overtime**, usually at a higher rate, e.g. **time and a half** means you get 1.5 hours' pay for each hour of overtime. **Minimum wage:** the least a full-time employee may legally be paid per hour.
2 **Piece rate:** you are paid for each item produced. Bricklayers are paid for each brick laid.
3 **Commission:** you get paid a certain percentage (%) of the value of goods that you sell. A bonus may be paid as well if certain targets are met.
4 **Salary:** you get paid a fixed sum per month to do a job, however long it takes to do it. Teachers, engineers and accountants are usually paid a salary.

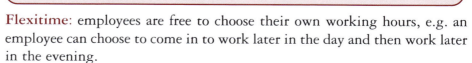

Tip

Remember

Gross Pay = Basic Pay + Overtime + Commission

Net Pay = Gross Pay − Deductions

Flexitime: employees are free to choose their own working hours, e.g. an employee can choose to come in to work later in the day and then work later in the evening.

Subsidised (e.g. subsidised canteen): An employer pays some of cost so the employees get cheaper food.

Sample Questions

1 Time rate

Bart is paid €7.50 per hour for a normal working week of 39 hours. Overtime is paid at time and a half. Last week Bart worked 45 hours. Calculate his gross pay.

Solution

45 – 39 = 6 hours overtime.
Time and a half: €7.50 × 1.5 = €11.25

Basic:	39 × €7.50	=	€292.50
+ Overtime:	6 × €11.25	=	€ 67.50
Gross pay		=	€360.00

2 Piece rate

Maebh is a seamstress and is paid €0.40 for every T-shirt she completes. This week she completed 1,412 T-shirts. How much will her gross pay be?

Solution

1,412 × €0.40 = €564.80

3 Commission

Donncha works in a sports shop. He is paid a basic wage of €50 per week and a commission of 5% of his total sales. Last week he sold €4,000 worth of goods. Calculate his gross pay.

Solution

5% of €4,000 =	€200
+ Basic	€50
Gross pay	€250

Income Tax Forms

P60

Given to the employee by the employer at the end of the year.
It shows the total pay, PAYE and PRSI for the year.

P45 Cessation Certificate

Given to an employee when he/she leaves a firm.

Payslip

We saw in Chapter 1 how to complete a payslip. A payslip like the one below is what the employee receives.

Wage Slip: **Mary Whyte**			Week 11	
PAY	**€**	**DEDUCTIONS**	**€**	
BASIC	252.00	PAYE	39.55	
OVERTIME	42.00	PRSI	19.95	
		SAVINGS	25.00	NET PAY
GROSS PAY	294.00	TOTAL DEDUCTIONS	84.50	209.50

A simple form of this exists, though it rarely makes an appearance in the exam.

Name	Basic €	O/Time €	Gross €	PAYE €	PRSI €	Savings €	Total Deductions €	Net Pay €
Mary Whyte	252.00	42.00	294.00	39.55	19.95	25.00	84.50	209.50

 **How to**

Wages Book

Employers need to keep a record of wages/salaries paid. This is done in the wages book. The total cost of wages and employer's PRSI is calculated. The information for the payslip is extracted from the wages book.

Sample Question

St Paul's Ink Ltd has two employees who are paid on a monthly basis. Each employee pays PRSI at the rate of 8%. The employer's rate of PRSI is 12%. Complete the wages book, for the month of May 2008 using the partially completed wages book.

Calculate the **total cost of wages** for the month of May 2008.

Solution

Date	Name	Gross Wages	PAYE	PRSI	Total	Net Wages	Employer's PRSI
31-05-08	Mary Black	1,855	600	148.40	748.40	1106.60	222.60
31-05-08	Luke Green	1,480	460	118.40	578.40	901.60	177.60
	Total	3,335	1060	266.80	1326.80	2008.20	400.20

The total cost of wages is the Total Gross Wages plus the employer's PRSI.
3,335 + 400.20 = €3,735.20

Workings

Mary Black
Employee PRSI
    8% of 1,855 = 148.40
Employer PRSI
    12% of 1,855 = 222.60

Luke Green
Employee PRSI
    8% of 1,480 = 118.40
Employer PRSI
    12% of 1,480 = 177.60

Payment of Wages and Salaries

Wages/salaries can be paid by cash, by cheque or by credit transfer. (PAYPATH).
Payment by cash is unusual nowadays.

Coin/Note Analysis

If wages are paid in cash, the employer needs to do a coin/note analysis. This gives a breakdown of how many of each coin/note will be required.

If St Paul's Ink Ltd paid their wages in cash, their coin/note analysis would look like this:

NAME	NET PAY	NOTES						COINS				
		200	100	50	20	10	5	2	1	50	20	10
Mary Black	1,106.60	5	1				1		1	1		1
Luke Green	901.60	4	1						1	1		1
Total	2,008.20	9	2				1		2	2		2

Questions

REVISE WISE
Q
QUESTIONS

Try these other questions

H '95 II B5

a) Name **two** rights and two responsibilities of an employer.

H '95 II 5

b) State **two** methods of calculating gross pay.

c) Oidar Ltd has three employees who are paid on a monthly basis. Each employee pays income tax (PAYE) at the rate of 30% of gross wages. The employer's PRSI is 12% of gross wages.

   i) Complete the wages book for the month of May 1995 using the partially completed wages book below.

   ii) Calculate the **total cost of wages** for Oidar Ltd for the month of May 1995.

Date	Name	Gross Wage	Deductions			Total	Net Wages	Employer's PRSI
			PAYE	PRSI	Pension			
		€	€	€	€	€	€	€
31-05	R. Kenny	1,600		112	80			
31-05	L. Dunne	1,400		98	70			
31-05	T. Doyle	1,200		84	60			
	Total							

Hiring Procedures	Rates of Pay	General
H '01 II5(a)	H '04 I B6(a,c)	H '04 I B6(b)
	H '06 I B4(b(i, ii))	H '00 I B6(a)
	H '06 II 3(b)	

CHAPTER 21
Industrial Relations

●●●**Learning Objectives**

Learn how to:

● state the steps in resolving industrial relations problems

Understand:

● role and types of trade unions
● role of the shop steward
● Irish Congress of Trades Unions

Tip

Tick each one off when you feel confident that you know it.

Definition

Industrial Relations describes the relationship between workers and management.

Good industrial relations helps productivity as workers are well motivated. Poor industrial relations can lead to absenteeism, low productivity and high labour turnover as unhappy workers leave.

 **Understand**

Trade Union

Definition

A group of workers joining together to secure better pay and working conditions.

Most unions are members of the Irish Congress of Trades Unions (ICTU).

Types of Union

Craft: members of a skilled trade, e.g. Brick and Stonelayers' Trade Union.
White Collar: members of a profession, e.g. Irish National Teachers' Organisation (INTO), Irish Nurses' Organisation (INO).
Industrial: workers in a particular industry, e.g. Irish Bank Officials' Association (IBOA).

General: workers from different occupations, e.g. Services, Industrial, Professional and Technical Union (SIPTU).

Functions
1 Negotiate improved wages/salaries for workers
2 Negotiate working conditions
3 Negotiate with management in case of a dispute
4 Negotiate conditions in case of redundancy
5 Protect from unfair dismissal
6 Negotiate with the government, through ICTU

Benefits of Joining
1 Improved standard of living
2 Improved job security
3 Legal help in case of dismissal

How to Join
1 Contact the *shop steward*
2 Complete *application form*
3 Pay *subscription*

Social Partnership/National Wage Agreements

ICTU represents the unions and the workers and IBEC (Irish Business Employers' Confederation) represents the employers.

In Ireland, ICTU, IBEC and the government agree to rates of pay increase, changes in tax and investment in the economy.

This helps the economy by minimizing the number of working days lost to strikes.

Industrial Disputes

Causes
- pay
- (unfair) dismissal
- working conditions (e.g. safety, canteen)
- demarcation (who does what)
- redundancy (letting workers go due to lack of work). Should be done on 'Last in First Out' basis (LIFO), meaning that the newest employees are the first to go.

Role of Management

- to represent the interests of the owners
- to keep the workers working
- if the management don't listen to the workers grievances (complaints), the dispute will get worse (escalate)

Types of Dispute

Work to rule: workers only do the minimum (i.e. no overtime, office staff might not answer the phone).

Go slow: workers do the job, but slowly.

Token stoppage: workers stop for a short time, e.g. a couple of hours or half a day.

Strike: work stops until the dispute is resolved.

- *official strike*
  - ○ Workers have legal protection
  - ○ Workers vote by secret ballot
  - ○ Employer gets a weeks' notice
  - ○ Workers may get strike pay from their union
- *unofficial strike*
  - ○ No notice is given
  - ○ Workers get no strike pay
- *all-out strike*
  - ○ All the unions in a workplace support the striking union. No member of an ICTU union will cross the picket

Your revision notes

How to

The Steps in Resolving a Dispute

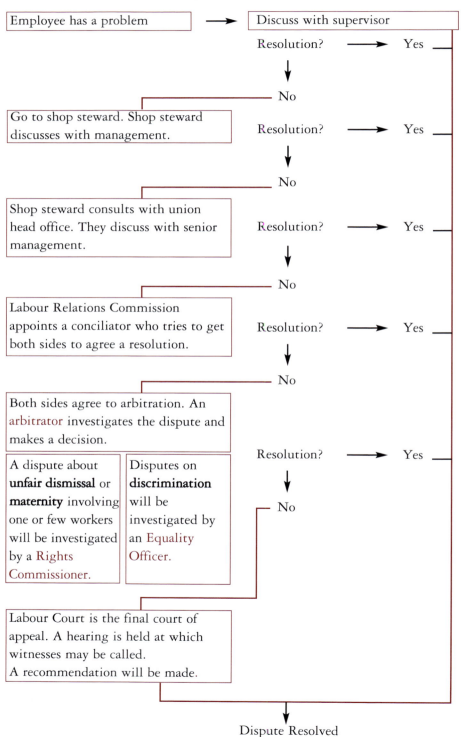

| Employee has a problem | → | Discuss with supervisor |

Resolution? → Yes

↓

No

Go to shop steward. Shop steward discusses with management.

Resolution? → Yes

↓

No

Shop steward consults with union head office. They discuss with senior management.

Resolution? → Yes

↓

No

Labour Relations Commission appoints a conciliator who tries to get both sides to agree a resolution.

Resolution? → Yes

↓

No

Both sides agree to arbitration. An arbitrator investigates the dispute and makes a decision.

Resolution? → Yes

↓

No

A dispute about **unfair dismissal** or **maternity** involving one or few workers will be investigated by a Rights Commissioner.

Disputes on **discrimination** will be investigated by an Equality Officer.

Labour Court is the final court of appeal. A hearing is held at which witnesses may be called.
A recommendation will be made.

Dispute Resolved

Questions

Try these other questions

H '94 I A 5

Give a short explanation of *each* of the following terms used in industrial relations:
Work to Rule and *Arbitration.*

H '99 I A 5

Place a tick (✔) opposite *each* statement to indicate whether it is true or false.
The labour force includes:

	True	False
a) SIPTU is the name of a trade union	☐	☐
b) AIB is the name of a trade union	☐	☐
c) IDA is the name of a trade union	☐	☐
d) INTO is the name of a trade union	☐	☐

H '96 II4

b) Give *three* reasons why strikes take place.
c) Study the newspaper report below and answer the questions that follow.
    i) What was the dispute about?
    ii) Name the two parties to the dispute.
    iii) What form of action did the union vote to take?
    iv) How might the dispute be settled?

> **Agricultural Staff Vote for Action**
> *Members of the Civil and Public Service Union in the offices of the Department of Agriculture have voted by four to one to implement industrial action because of what it calls the Department's breach of an agreement on the employment of temporary staff.*
> *The action includes a ban on overtime, refusal to perform duties appropriate to higher grades, and a ban on telephone and public office queries.*

Questions

H '06 I B4(a)   H '02 I B4b, c(i)   H '00 I B6b

H '03 II 3

CHAPTER 22

Formation of a Private Limited Company

●●●Learning Objectives

Learn how to:

● prepare Memorandum and Articles of Association from information given

Understand:

● documents (certificate of incorporation, memorandum and articles of association, declaration of compliance, statement of capital)
● auditor, board of directors, registrar of companies

Tip

Tick each one off when you feel confident that you know it.

Understand

Forming a Company

There are 7 steps to take in forming a company.

1 1–50 investors (shareholders) come together and decide:
● what the company is to do
● what it is to be named
● how much each will invest

2 They appoint
● directors
● an accountant
● a solicitor

3 They prepare certain documents:
  i *Memorandum of Association*
 ii *Articles of Association*
iii *Declaration of Compliance*
 iv *Statement of Capital of the Company*

4 The documents are sent to **The Registrar of Companies**.

5 The Registrar issues a **Certificate of Incorporation**. This is the company's 'Birth Certificate' and identifies it as being separate from its owners. It can sue (and be sued) and can be in debt independently. This is what gives limited liability.

6 A bank account is opened in the company name.

7 The company begins trading.

 **How to**

Sample Question

On the 29 February 2008, Caoimhe McCooey of The Pilotage, Arklow, County Wicklow, and Stephen McGee of 22 Portview, Arklow, County Wicklow formed a Private Limited Company called St Paul's Ink Ltd. They prepared a Memorandum of Association and Articles of Association and sent it, and all the other necessary documents, to the Registrar of Companies. A Certification of Incorporation was then issued.

The objects of the company are to manufacture, distribute and sell ink and ink products to the education sector.

The Authorised Share Capital of St Paul's Ink Ltd is 500,000 €1 ordinary shares. On 5 March 2008, Caoimhe McCooey purchased 55,000 shares and Stephen McGee purchased 40,000 shares.

a) From the information given, draft the Articles of Association for St Paul's Ink. Ltd.

b) Complete the blank Memorandum of Association given, using the information supplied above.

Answer

Articles of Association of St Paul's Ink Ltd	
Name of company	St Paul's Ink Ltd
Details of Share Capital	Share Capital of the company is €500,000 divided into 500,000 shares of €1 each
Shareholders' voting rights	Shareholders have one vote per share
Regulation as to general meetings	AGM to be held on the first Monday of July
How directors are to be elected	The directors will be elected at the AGM and will hold office for 1 year
Powers & duties of directors	The directors will be responsible for the day-to-day running of the company
Borrowing powers of the company	The company may borrow up to €500,000
How the company will be wound up	If the company becomes insolvent, it will be wound up
Names of directors	Name Address Stephen McGee Arklow Caoimhe McCooey Arklow
Date	29 Feb 2008
Signed	S McGee
	C McCooey
Witnessed	H O'Rahilly

Tip

The Articles of Association set out the way the company will relate to the world outside

Tip

It is more important that all the information is present than that it is in the right order.

Answer

MEMORANDUM OF ASSOCIATION

1. The name of the company is   *St Paul's Ink Ltd*

2. The objects for which the company is established are:
Manufacture, distribute and sell ink products to the educational sector

3. The liability of members is limited

4. The share capital of the company is *€500,000* divided
into *€1 shares*

We the several persons whose names, addresses and descriptions are subscribed wish to be formed into a Company in pursuance of the Memorandum of Association and we agree to take the number of shares in the Capital of the Company set opposite our names

Name, Address of each subscriber	Number of shares taken by each subscriber
Caoimhe McCooey *The Pilotage, Arklow* *Co. Wicklow*	*55,000*
Stephen McGee *22 Portview, Arklow* *Co. Wicklow*	*40,000*

Date   *29/02/2008*

Tip
The Memorandum of
Association sets out
how the company is to be run.

Tip
If either of these documents is asked in an exam, you will probably
be given a blank form to complete.

Understand

People in the Formation of the Business

Promoter: The initial shareholders, the 'founders'.

Board of Directors: Appointed by the shareholders for the day-to-day running of the business.

Auditor: An accountant appointed by the shareholders to confirm the accuracy of the accounts.

Registrar of Companies: Makes sure no competing businesses use the same name. Makes sure companies comply with the law and issues Certificate of Incorporation.

Question

H '98 II 2b,c

On 1 May 1998, Maria Burke of 4 Bridge St, Athlone, County Westmeath and Mike Mitchell of 10 Shannon View, Athlone, County Westmeath formed a Private Limited Company called AT YOUR SERVICE LTD. They prepared a Memorandum of Association and sent it and all the other necessary documents to the Registrar of Companies. A Certificate of Incorporation was then issued. The objects of the company are to provide computer and secretarial services. The authorised share capital of AT YOUR SERVICE LTD is 80,000 €1 ordinary shares.

On 10 May 1998, Maria Burke purchased 20,000 shares and Mike Mitchell purchased 15,000 shares.

b) Complete the Memorandum of Association below. (14 marks)

c) Name **two** other documents which should be sent to the Registrar of Companies when forming a private limited company. (6 marks)

MEMORANDUM OF ASSOCIATION

1. The name of the company is _____

2. The objects for which the company is established are:

_____

_____

3. The liability of members is limited

4. The share capital of the company is_____ divided into_____

We the several persons whose names, addresses and descriptions are subscribed wish to be formed into a Company in pursuance of the Memorandum of Association and we agree to take the number of shares in the Capital of the Company set opposite our names

Name, Address of each subscriber	Number of shares taken by each subscriber

Date --

Questions

Try these other questions

H '04 I A4   H '02 II 3b(i)

●●●**Learning Objectives**

Learn how to:

- identify target market
- select appropriate method of promotion

Understand:

- 4 Ps of marketing mix
- advertising; media, types, steps in designing a campaign
- branding, special offers, public relations
- market research, types of market

Tip

Tick each one off when you feel confident that you know it.

 **Understand**

Definitions

Market Everybody who might be interested in buying something. (also the place where buying and selling happens).

Types of Market
    Retail market Goods and Services sold to the public.
    Wholesale market Goods and Services sold to retailers.
    Export market Goods and Services sold abroad.
    Stock market (stock exchange) Shares in companies bought and sold.
    Import substitution A good made in Ireland to compete with an imported good.

Market Segmentation The market is divided into people with something in common (e.g. same age, same country, same hobbies).

Target Market The market segment you want to sell to. You may sell a slightly different product to the different segments (e.g. Pepsi, Pepsi Max, Diet Pepsi, Pepsi Twist).

The target market for this book is Junior Certificate Business Studies students.

Marketing

Definition The process of finding out what customers want, and selling it to them.

Market Research
Successful marketing begins with market research.

What to find out
- what customers want
- who your customers are
- how much they are willing to pay
- what your competitors are doing

How to find out

Desk Research
- looking at information already in your files, or from published sources (e.g. census).

Field Research
- collecting new information by:
- questionnaire (on the internet, in magazines)
- interview (in person, by phone)
- focus group (a small group of customers discuss the product)
- observation (watching and recording customer behaviour)

Marketing Mix

(The 4 Ps of Marketing)

Promotion

Place   Product

Price

Product
- the good or service that you make
- product development

New product ideas come from:
- – customers (complaints, suggestions, requests)
- – staff (suggestions, research and development)
- – improving on existing products

Price
- how much you charge
- must cover all costs (including development)
- must provide a profit
- must be low enough to compete

Place
- the channel of distribution
- where the product will be available

Promotion

Techniques used to encourage customers to buy.

1 Advertising

Types

Informative Advertising (information on price, features, availability)
Persuasive Advertising (convince the customer)
Competitive Advertising (compare product with competitor)
Generic Advertising (An industry promoting a product, e.g. 'Eat more Beef').

Functions
- to inform
- to persuade
- to present an image of the company

Media (where to advertise)
- newspapers/magazines
- leaflets/flyers
- posters/billboards
- buses/trains/taxis
- sporting events
- radio/television
- internet
- cinema
- window displays
- trade fairs
- shopping bags

Creating an advertising campaign

Identify your target market.

Identify your message (what you want to say).

This will help you decide:
- the type; and
- the medium

A good advertisement
- attracts attention
- informs the customer
- reaches the target market
- encourages action (i.e. buy this)

Advertising is also used to get people to change their behaviour, e.g. 'stop smoking', 'slow down', 'get more exercise'. The above points apply to this type of advertising also.

2 Sales Promotion
- free samples
- special offers
- coupons/tokens
- competitions/gifts

3 Public Relations
- publicity for the company
- supporting community events

4 Sponsorship
- sponsoring sport teams (e.g. Supermacs and the Galway football team)
- sponsoring competitions (e.g. Texaco Children's Art Competition)

5 Selling techniques
- branding, trademarks, logos

A **brand** is a company name used to distinguish a product from competitors, e.g. Mercedes.

A **trademark** is the company's product name and the way it is written, e.g. Apple Computers.

A **logo** is a symbol for a product or the company.

Merchandising

The way products are displayed to catch the eye.

Questions

Try these questions

H '98 II 6

a) State three reasons why a business carries out market research. (9 marks)

b) Explain two methods (techniques) of obtaining information about a market. (10 marks)

c) Describe two suitable advertising media for promoting food. (8 marks)

H '94 I A19

Name the four P's of marketing

1 _____

2 _____

3 _____

4 _____

H '98 I A 2

A firm wishes to launch a new product. From the following list of activities to be undertaken, indicate by means of a tick (✓) which of the sequences below is the correct one.

1 Sales Promotion	a) 3 1 4 2	☐
2 Retail Sales	b) 4 2 1 3	☐
3 Product Development	c) 3 4 2 1	☐
4 Market Research	d) 4 3 1 2	☐
	e) 4 1 3 2	☐

H '04 II 3	H '03 I A13
H '02 I A5	H '01 I A2
H '06 I A4	H '06 I A10
H '06 II 6(a)	

●●●Learning Objectives

Learn how to:

- select a delivery system
- calculate delivery times/costs

Understand:

- road, rail, air, sea, pipeline
- cost, speed, reliability, safety, distance, suitability
- transport terms
- containers, refrigerated transport
- fixed and variable costs

Tip

Tick each one off when you feel confident that you know it.

Understand

Transport Terms

Containers: Standard size metal boxes in which goods are packed. They reduce the time required of a truck or ship to load and unload.

Lo-Lo: A ship where cargo is lifted on and off by crane.

Ro-Ro: A ship where cargo is driven on and off by truck (e.g. car ferry)

Refrigerated transport: Where the goods are kept at a low temperature. Perishable goods (meat, fruit, vegetables) can be taken long distances.

Ex-Works: Buyer pays all delivery cost.

CIF: Carriage, Insurance and Freight. Price quoted includes all costs to the port of destination.

C & F: Carriage and Freight. Price quoted includes all costs to the port of destination except insurance.

FOB: Free On Board. Price quoted includes all costs to the port of boarding only.

	Road	Rail	Sea	Air	Pipeline
Cost *the price*	Medium cost per km, low handling costs.	Low cost per km, higher handling costs.	Low cost per km.	Very expensive per km.	Very expensive to build, very cheap to use.
Speed *how soon will it get there?*	Medium to slow.	Fast to Medium.	Slow.	Very fast.	Fast and continuous.
Flexibility *different addresses or different size loads*	Anywhere in Ireland. Needs sea/air to deliver outside Ireland. Can go anytime. Small loads (40t).	Limited routes. Some restriction on time. Large loads (1000t).	Only coastal destinations and certain waterways (Rhine, Mississippi). Very large loads (20000t).	Limited routes. Limited timetable. Small Loads(100t).	Fixed route (Dublin City Council water pipes delivers 435000 t per day).
Reliability *will it get there when I want?*	Traffic can cause delays.	Major delays are rare.	Bad weather can delay a ship or stop it sailing.	Most flights go as scheduled.	Breakdowns are very rare.
Safety *will it get there at all?*	Safe, but theft a risk for certain high-value goods (e.g. money, cigarettes).	Very safe.	Goods may be damaged in a storm.	Very safe.	Very Safe.
Distance	Best for short distances.	Cost of handling makes short distances expensive.	Best for long distances if speed is not important.	Better for long distances.	Best over any distance where continuous supply is needed.
Suitability *what can I send?*	Good for people and non-bulky goods.	People and bulky goods. May need to use road for part of journey so more handling.	Too slow over long distances. Containers help reduce handling costs.	People and small, high-value items (e.g. computer parts).	Liquids and gases only.

Bulky goods = Coal, wheat, for example

Handling = Cost of loading and unloading

How to

Calculating delivery time and cost

Delivery Time = Distance (km) ÷ Average Speed (km/h)
In the exam, you may be given the distance or you may have to read it from a distance table.

Cavan

300	Cork					
110	400	**Donegal**				
111	260	222	Dublin			
82	325	158	85	Dundalk		
199	142	260	230	256	Ennis	
166	210	205	216	238	70	**Galway**

The distance from Donegal to Galway is 205 km.

Sample Question

A courier travels from Cavan to Ennis. She then delivers a packet to a firm in Dublin before returning to Cavan. How many kilometres does she travel altogether? Travelling at an average speed of 60 kilometres per hour, how long will the journey take?

Solution

Cavan to Ennis	199 km
Ennis to Dublin	230 km
Dublin to Cavan	111 km
Total = (199+230+111) =	540 km

Distance/Average Speed = 540/60 = 9 hours

Delivery Cost

A business needs to choose the least expensive form of transport available.

Using own vehicle

Fixed costs: paid however much vehicles are used.

Divided by a number of working days (maintenance, tax, insurance).

Variable costs: depend on how much the vehicle is used. May be calculated per km, per day or per hour.

Tip

Anything with 'annual' in it is a fixed cost.

Advantages of using your own delivery vehicles

- always available
- advertising on vehicle
- can take return loads

Your revision notes

Sample Question

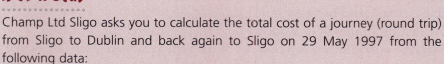

H'97 II 5(d)

Champ Ltd Sligo asks you to calculate the total cost of a journey (round trip) from Sligo to Dublin and back again to Sligo on 29 May 1997 from the following data:

- the distance from Sligo to Dublin is 217km
- the diesel vehicle can do 14km per litre of diesel
- the cost of diesel is 50c per litre
- the van driver's wages are €75 per day
- the annual motor tax is €450
- the annual motor insurance is €1,200
- the annual repairs are €600
- Champ Ltd operates 300 working days in the year

Solution

Fixed Costs   €

	€
Annual Motor Tax	450
Annual Motor Insurance	1,200
Annual Repairs	600
	2,250

Fixed Costs per day = 2,250/300 = €7.50 per day

Variable Costs

Sligo to Dublin	217 km
and Back	217 km
Total Distance	434 km

Fuel used = 434/14 = 31 litres

Cost of Fuel 31 x 50c = €15.50

Total Cost

Fixed Cost	7.50
Fuel	15.50
Driver	75.00
Total Cost	98.00

Using a Courier

Collection Fee paid to have goods picked up.

Delivery Fee usually per kg to deliver to a certain area (e.g. within Limerick city).

Sample Question

A car parts supplier needs to send a parcel weighing 20kg from Galway to Sligo. He wishes to use a courier. Calculate the costs. Quick 'n' Safe quotes the following:

	Galway	Rest of Connaught
Collection Fee	€45.00	€55.00
Fee per kg	€1.30	€1.90

Solution

Collection Fee	€45.00	(Goods Collected in Galway)
Fee per kg	€38.00	(20kg x €1.90)
Total Costs	€83.00	

Questions

Try these other questions

H '97 II 5(b)

Transport is very important in the distribution of goods.

Explain **three** factors that should be taken into account when deciding on the type of delivery system to be used by a business. (9 marks)

H '99 II 6(a,b,c)

a) Give **three reasons** why transport is important in the chain of distribution. (6 marks)

b) State and explain **three factors** which affect the choice of delivery system used by a business. (9 marks)

c) Calculate the cost of transport for **one day** from the following details provided by Jump Ltd:

- Jump Ltd operates 300 working days in the year
- the diesel van can travel 18km per litre
- the distance travelled in one day is 648km
- the cost of diesel is 50c per litre
- the van driver's wages are €85 per day
- the Annual Motor Tax is €510
- the Annual Motor Insurance is €1,350
- the Annual Repairs are €840

H '01 II 6(a)   H '03 II 5(a,b,c)
H '03 I A4   H '02 I A9
H '01 I A4

●●●**Learning Objectives**

Learn how to:

- trace a transaction from order to payment
- carry out simple stock control

Understand:

- letter of enquiry, quotation, order, delivery docket, invoice, debit note, credit note, statement of account and receipt
- the importance of stock control

Tip

Tick each one off when you feel confident that you know it.

A business must keep records of all its dealings. When buying and selling, it is best to have a written record so that the buyer and seller can be certain of what is being bought and sold, and of the price.

Most businesses buy and sell on credit, rather than paying cash. They usually get 30 days' credit. This means that they must pay for the goods within 30 days. The advantage of this to a business is that it gives them a chance to get cash for the goods by selling them to a consumer for cash. Then they have the cash to pay for the goods.

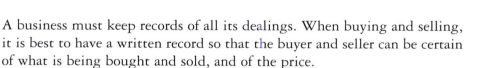

Business documents has been examined almost every year on paper II. The questions generally ask you to complete a document from information supplied.

 **Understand**

Business Documents

1 A business decides it wants to buy something and sends a **letter of enquiry** to a number of suppliers

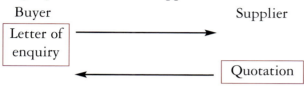

Buyer   Supplier

Letter of enquiry →

← Quotation

2 Suppliers send back a quotation setting out the price and any **conditions of sale**

3 The business compares the quotations and picks the best one (usually the lowest price that can supply all the goods). An **order form** is sent to the supplier

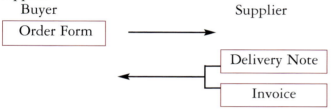

Buyer   Supplier

Order Form →

← Delivery Note

Invoice

4 The supplier checks to make sure the goods are in stock and makes up the order

5 The goods are delivered, along with two documents:
   - **delivery note**: details what goods were delivered
   - **invoice**: details the price. This is the bill

   After checking the goods, the *purchasing manager* signs to say that the goods have been delivered.

6 If the buyer is a regular customer, the supplier will send a **statement of account** at the end of each month

7 Payment by cheque is sent to the supplier

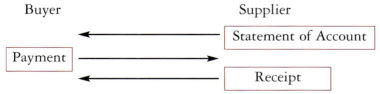

Buyer   Supplier

← Statement of Account

Payment →

← Receipt

8 The supplier sends back a **receipt** acknowledging payment has been received

 **How to**

Letter of Enquiry

St. Paul's Ink Ltd want to buy packing boxes. They send a **letter of enquiry**. The letter may be sent to more than one supplier

---

No.: 01234

St Paul's Ink Ltd
Shy Bill Hill
Arklow
County Wicklow
Tel: 0402 1234567
Fax: 0402 1234568
E-mail: *stpaul@eircom.net*
VAT Reg. No. 782910R

Mike's Box Co Ltd
Carrigaline Business Park
County Cork

29 August 2009

Dear Sir or Madam,

Please send a quotation for the following goods:

150 Euro boxes size A
200 Euro boxes size B
20 Euro boxes size F

Yours sincerely

Stephen Mc Gee
Purchasing Manager

Tip

The number on each document is a filing number for the company sending the document.

Quotation

St Paul's Ink Ltd received quotations from several companies, including this one.

- the price given on the quotation must be honoured for the period stated on it
- delivery is when the goods will be available, e.g. ready/immediate, 1 week, etc

Quotation 311

Mike's Box Co Ltd
Carrigaline Business Park
Carrigaline
County Cork
Ph: 021 361224
VAT Reg No.: 321684Q

St Paul's Ink Ltd
Shy Bill Hill
Arklow
County Wicklow

04 September 2009

Dear Sir,

Thank you for your enquiry. Our quotation is as follows:

Quantity	Description	Unit	Delivery
150	Euro boxes size A	€45 per 50	Immediate
200	Euro boxes size B	€80 per 50	Immediate
20	Euro boxes size F	€40 per 10	1 week

All prices valid for one month.

Yours sincerely

Rick Fraser
Sales Manager

Terms of Sale:
VAT 20%. Trade Discount 10%. Carriage Paid.

Terms of Sale
- is VAT included or not and at what rate?
- trade discount
- period of credit given
- carriage paid by whom?

COD = Cash On Delivery
CWO = Cash With Order

Order

You set out what you want to order. You may choose to order goods from a number of different suppliers.

Order 36

St Paul's Ink Ltd
Shy Bill Hill
Arklow
County Wicklow
Tel: 0402 1234567
Fax: 0402 1234568
E-mail: stpaul@eircom.net
VAT Reg. No. 782910R

Mike's Box Co Ltd
Carrigaline Business Park
Carrigaline
County Cork

06 September 2009

Please supply the following goods as per Quotation 311:

Quantity	Description	Unit
150	Euro boxes size A	€45 per 50
200	Euro boxes size B	€80 per 50
20	Euro boxes size F	€40 per 10

For delivery to the above address within 14 days.

Signed

Stephen McGee
Purchasing Manager

When Mike's Box Co Ltd receives the order, they take the following action:

1 Put the date received on it
2 Prepare the order
3 Send the order form to the office to prepare the invoice and delivery docket
4 File it

Delivery Note

This details goods actually delivered.

It is a duplicate (carbon copy) document that St Paul's Ink sign to say the goods were delivered in good order.

In practice it is usual to sign for goods and inspect them later.

Delivery Note 264

Mike's Box Co Ltd
Carrigaline Business Park
Carrigaline
County Cork
Ph: 021 361224
VAT Reg No.: 321684Q

Order No. 36
St Paul's Ink Ltd
Shy Bill Hill
Arklow
County Wicklow

Quantity	Description
150	Euro boxes size A
200	Euro boxes size B
20	Euro boxes size F

Received the above goods in good condition.

Signed

Stephen McGee
Purchasing Manager

Invoice

This is the bill.

It may accompany the delivery or it may be posted out later.

E.&O.E. means Errors and Omissions Excepted, i.e. if any mistakes are made in calculating the invoice, they can be corrected.

Invoice 233

Mike's Box Co Ltd
Carrigaline Business Park
Carrigaline
County Cork

10 September 2009
Ref Order 36

Quantity	Description	Unit Price	Total
150	Euro boxes size A	€40 per 50	€120
200	Euro boxes size B	€80 per 50	€320
20	Euro boxes size F	€40 per 10	€80
	Total (ex VAT)		€520
	Less Trade Discount		€52
			€468
	Add VAT		€93.60
	Total		**€561.60**

E.&O.E.

Correcting Errors

A **Debit Note** is sent if:

The supplier *undercharges* for some items on the invoice.

The supplier *omits some items* from the invoice.

A **Credit Note** is sent if:

The supplier *overcharges*.

The buyer *returns goods* to the supplier (e.g. faulty goods).

Tip

A Debit Note *increases* the sum owed.
A Credit Note *reduces* the sum owed.

Debit Note

The Debit Note will describe what the error was and calculate the additional amount due.

Tip

Remember, calculate the discount *before* VAT

Debit Note 12

Mike's Box Co Ltd
Carrigaline Business Park
Carrigaline
County Cork

St Paul's Ink Ltd
Shy Bill Hill
Arklow
County Wicklow

12 September 2009

Quantity	Description	Unit Price	Total
150	Euro boxes size A	€5 per 50	€15
	Less Trade Discount		€1.50
			€13.50
	Add VAT (20%)		€2.70
	Total		**€16.20**

Undercharging on Invoice 233

Credit Note

The credit note will describe what the error was and calculate the reduction or refund.

Remember, calculate the discount *before* VAT

Credit Note 47

Mike's Box Co Ltd
Carrigaline Business Park
Carrigaline
County Cork

St Paul's Ink Ltd
Shy Bill Hill
Arklow
County Wicklow

12 September 2009

Quantity	Description	Unit Price	Total
50	Euro boxes size B	€80 per 50	€80
	Less Trade Discount		€8
			€72
	Add VAT (20%)		€14.40
	Total		**€86.40**

Faulty Goods (moisture damage) ref. Invoice 233

Statement of Account

A **statement of account** is sent to each debtor at the end of the month. It will show a list of invoices, debit and credit notes and payments received and the amount outstanding (the balance due).

Statement of Account No. 212

Mike's Box Co Ltd
Carrigaline Business Park
Carrigaline
County Cork
Ph 021 361244
VAT Reg. No.: 321684Q

St Paul's Ink Ltd
Shy Bill Hill
Arklow
County Wicklow

12 September 2009

Date	Details	Debit	Credit	Balance
10 Sep	Invoice 233	€561.60		€561.60
12 Sep	Debit Note 12	€16.20		€577.80
20 Sep	Credit Note 47		€86.40	€491.40
	Amount Due			€491.40

Payment

Payment is usually made by cheque. Business cheques are signed by two people, usually the treasurer/cashier and the secretary.

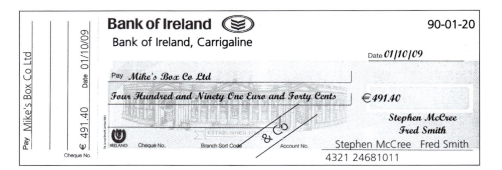

Receipt

A receipt is usually a duplicate docket acknowledging the payment has been received.

It is filed along with the invoice being paid.

Receipt: 324

Mike's BOX CO Ltd

8 Oct 2009

Received with thanks

The sum of   _Four hundred and ninety-one euro 40 cent_

€491.40

From: St.Paul's Ink Ltd

Shy Bill Hill

Arklow

County Wicklow

Signed _K. Shelly_

Accounts Department

Understand

Stock Control

Stock Control means managing how much 'goods for resale' you have at any time.

It is important because:

1 If you run out of something you may lose customers, as you will not be able to meet orders

2 If you have too much stock, it may break, rust, go off or out of fashion or be stolen before you can sell it

3 It costs money to keep stock in a warehouse

Stocktaking

Why?

● to find closing stock
● to identify stock not selling well
● to identify damaged/out-of-date stock
● to identify theft

How?

● close the shop/warehouse
● count and record how many units of each item you have
● accounts department values the stock and reports on damaged/missing or slow-selling stock

> **Tip**
>
> Stock is usually valued at the lowest of cost price, replacement price and selling price.

Your revision notes

Questions

Try these other questions

H '95 II 2 (c)

Durkin Shoes Ltd started up business on 1 June 1994 and ordered the following goods from Nobarry Ltd, Kelly Road, Cork.

20 pairs of Wellingtons	@IR£7 a pair
30 pairs of ladies' fashion boots	@IR£14 a pair
10 pairs of basketball trainers	@IR£17 a pair

Assume you are Nora Durkin, Purchasing Manager. Complete the **Order Form** on the blank order document:

ORDER NO: 271
DURKIN SHOES LTD
MAIN STREET
Carlow
Tel: (0503) 71189
VAT No IE 46611

Date:

To:

Please supply as per Quotation No. 989 the following:

Quantity	Description	Unit Price IR£

Goods to be delivered to above address within 10 days.

Signature
Position

H '96 II 2(b)

On 15 March 1996, ADAMS Electrical Ltd, Baggot St, Dublin 2, sent an order No. 5 to STONE Ltd Electrical Suppliers, Limerick, for the following goods:

12	SM Walkmans	@IR£15 each excluding VAT
4	True Colour TVs	@IR£455 each excluding VAT
8	VJ Video Recorders	@IR£250 each including VAT

STONE Ltd sent an invoice No. 18 on 22 March 1996.

This invoice, which ADAMS Electrical Ltd received on 23 March 1996, stated that the trade discount would be 25% of the retail price and that the goods would be delivered on 28 March 1996. Electrical goods are subject to VAT at 21%.

Complete the invoice of 22 March 1996

INVOICE
STONE LTD No. 18
ELECTRICAL SUPPLIERS
LIMERICK Tel. (061) 47231
VAT Reg. IE 112345

Date:
To:
Order No.:

Quantity	Description	Unit Price IR£	Total (Ex VAT) IR£

Less: Trade Discount
Add: VAT
Total
E&OE

H '00 II 2 b   *H '97 I A 6*   *H '05 II 2 a,b,c*

H '01 II 2 c   *H '04 II 2 a,b*

H '02 II 5 b,c   *H '03 II 2 b*

H '06 II 2(6(i,ii))

H '06 I A 6

CHAPTER 26
The Accounting Process (Purchases and Sales)

●●● **Learning Objectives**

Learn how to:

- enter figures from a source document in the appropriate book

Understand:

- what goes in each of the following: Purchases Day Book, Purchases Returns Day Book, Sales Day Book, Sales Return Day Book
- folio column shows the destination for posting

Tip

Tick each one off when you feel confident that you know it.

The information from invoices, credit notes and debit notes is summarised in the Books of First Entry.

 **Understand**

Which Day Book to use depends on:

1 Cash or credit transactions
2 The type of transaction

Tip

All cash and bank transactions will be recorded in the Cash Book (*see chapter 27*).

Credit Transactions are recorded as follows:

Book of First Entry	Nature of Transaction	Source Document
Purchases Day Book	Goods *for resale* purchased on credit	Invoices received
Purchases Returns Day Book	Goods for resale returned to seller (Returns Out)	Credit note received
Sales Day Book	Sales of stock	Invoice issued (sent)
Sales Returns Day Book	Goods previously sold returned by buyer (Returns In)	Credit note issued

Tip

All other credit transactions are recorded in the General Journal (*see chapter 29*).

Tip

The layout of the Purchases, Purchases Returns, Sales and Sales Returns Day Books is exactly the same.
Because of this, it is important to make sure to label each Day Book clearly.

 **How to**

Sample Question
(from H '95 II 1b)

The following transactions took place during the month of May 1995:

04/05/95   Purchased goods on credit from Ring Ltd   Invoice No. 39
            €12,000 + VAT at 21%
07/05/1995 Purchased goods on credit from Fitt Ltd   Invoice No. 17
            €7,600 + VAT at 21%
09/05/1995 Returned goods to Ring Ltd   Credit Note No. 17
            €1,600 + VAT at 21%

Record the transactions for the month of May 1995 in the appropriate books of first entry.

Solution

Remember to include the name of the day book

The value of the goods excluding tax

NET + VAT

What page in what ledger?

The tax paid (in €)

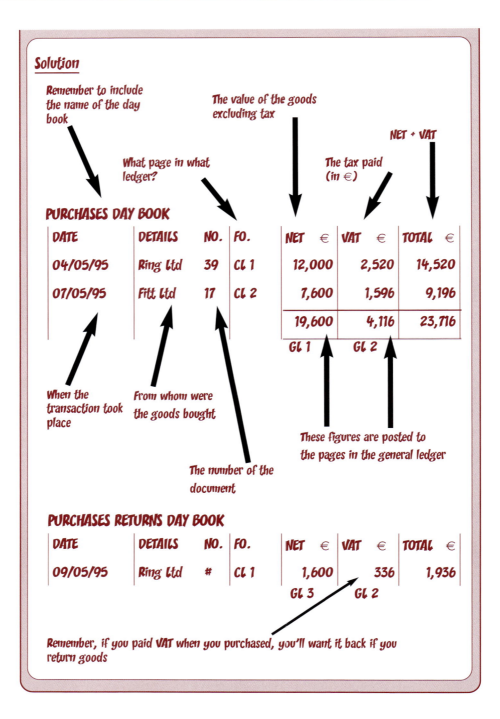

PURCHASES DAY BOOK

DATE	DETAILS	NO.	FO.	NET €	VAT €	TOTAL €
04/05/95	Ring Ltd	39	CL 1	12,000	2,520	14,520
07/05/95	Fitt Ltd	17	CL 2	7,600	1,596	9,196
				19,600	4,116	23,716
				GL 1	GL 2	

When the transaction took place

From whom were the goods bought

The number of the document

These figures are posted to the pages in the general ledger

PURCHASES RETURNS DAY BOOK

DATE	DETAILS	NO.	FO.	NET €	VAT €	TOTAL €
09/05/95	Ring Ltd	#	CL 1	1,600	336	1,936
				GL 3	GL 2	

Remember, if you paid **VAT** when you purchased, you'll want it back if you return goods

Questions

Try these other questions

H '95 1A9

Indicate, by means of a tick (✓), the correct answer to the following.

Credit notes received are the *Source Documents* for writing up the:

Purchases Returns Day Book ☐

Sales Returns Day Book ☐

Purchases Day Book ☐

H '97 1A13

Column 1 is a list of day books.

Column 2 is a list of source documents.

Match the two lists by placing the letter of the correct document under the number of the relevant book.

(One source document does not apply)

Column 1 Day Books	Column 2 Source documents
1 Sales Book	A Copy of credit note issued to customers
2 Purchases Returns Book	B Copy of receipts issued to customers
3 Sales Returns Book	C Credit note received from suppliers
4 Cheque Payments Book	D Counterfoil of cheque book
	E Copy of invoices issued to customers

1	2	3	4

H '98 II 1(a)

The following transactions took place during the month of May 1998.

		Inv No	
01/05/98	Purchased goods on credit from Top Ltd	Inv No 40	€16,000 + VAT at 12½%
06/05/98	Purchased goods on credit from Bot Ltd	Inv No 12	€21,200 + VAT at 12½%
10/05/98	Sold goods on credit to Mid Ltd	Inv No 1	€31,200 + VAT at 12½%

Record the transactions for the month of May 1998 in the appropriate Books of First Entry.

CHAPTER 27
Cash Book

●●● **Learning Objectives**

Learn how to:

● enter figures from source documents in the appropriate book

Understand:

● source documents; cheque stub;
lodgement slip
● what goes in the Cash Book

Tip

Tick each one off when you feel confident that you know it.

Tip

All transactions involving cash or cheques are recorded in the Cash Book.

The Cash Book may be presented in either of two ways:

Understand

Method 1 (Modern)

Analysed Cash Receipts and Lodgements Book.
Analysed Cash and Cheque Payments Book.
plus A *Cash Account* and a *Bank Account* in the General Ledger.

Method 2 (Traditional)

The two books are combined as a single book: The Analysed Cash Book.
In this method, there are no separate cash and bank accounts, the balances are taken from the Analysed Cash Book.
The Analysed Cash Book for a business is exactly the same as a household Analysed Cash Book (*see chapter four*). The analysis headings will vary from business to business.

Source Documents for the Cash Book

Cash Receipts	Cash register tally roll
	Copies of customers' receipts
Bank Lodgements	Bank lodgement counterfoils
Cash Payments	Cash vouchers show how the money was spent
Cheque Payments	Cheque counterfoils

Tip

It is unusual these days for a firm to make large cash payments. Payments by cheque are more secure and it is easier to prove that payment has been made.

Your revision notes

How to

Sample Question

Complete and balance the Analysed Cash Book (Analysed Receipts and Payments Book) of St. Paul's Ink Ltd for the month of May 2008 from the data below:

Use the following money column headings:

Debit (Receipts) side: Bank; Sales; VAT; Debtors.

Credit (Payments) side: Bank; Purchases; VAT; Creditors; Light & Heat; Wages.

			€
01/05/08	Balance		1,580
03/05	Cash sale lodged (including €1,000 in VAT)	Receipt no.5	6,000
08/05	College Crayons Ltd (debtor) settled their account by cheque and this was lodged	Receipt 6	€23,140
14/05	Paid wages by cheque	Cheque no. 9	12,000
19/05	Purchased stock (including €120 in VAT)	Cheque no. 10	600
22/05	Cash sale lodged (including €1,440 in VAT)	Receipt 7	7,600
27/05	Paid ESB by cheque	Cheque no.11	350
28/05	Paid wages by cheque	Cheque no.12	12,000
30/05	Jones Ltd (debtor) settled their account by cheque and this was lodged	Receipt no. 8	6,130
31/05	Paid Ceres Ltd, Creditor	Cheque no.13	1,450

Solution
Method 1 (Modern)
Analysed Cash Receipts and Lodgements Book

Date	Details	Fo.	Receipt no.	Bank	Sales	VAT	Debtors
03/05	Sales		5	6,000	5,000	1,000	
08/05	College Crayons Ltd		6	23,140			23,140
22/05	Sales		7	7,600	6,160	1,440	
30/05	Jones Ltd		8	6,130			6,130
				42,870	11,160	2,440	29,270

Analysed Cash and Cheque Payments Book

Date	Details	Fo.	Chq no.	Bank	Purchases	VAT	Creditors	Light & Heat	Wages
14/05	Wages		9	12,000					12,000
19/05	Purchases		10	600	480	120			
27/05	ESB		11	350				350	
28/05	Wages		12	12,000					12,000
31/05	Ceres Ltd		13	1,450			1,450		
				26,300	480	120	1,450	350	24,000

General Ledger
Bank Account

Date	Details	Fo.	€	Date	Details	Fo.	€
01/05	Balance	b/d	1,580	31/05	Payments		26,300
31/05	Receipts		42,870		Balance		18,150
			44,450				44,450
01/06	Balance	b/d	18,150				

Tip

A balance on the debit side of the bank account means you have money in the bank.
A balance on the credit side of the bank account means that you have an overdraft.

Alternative Answer

Solution

Method 2 (Traditional)

Analysed Cash Book

Date	Details	Fo.	no.	Bank	Sales	VAT	Debtors	Date	Details	Fo.	Chq no.	Bank	Purchases	VAT	Creditors	Light & Heat	Wages
01/05	Balance	b/d		1,580				14/05	Wages		9	12,000					12,000
03/05	Sales		5	6,000	5,000	1,000		19/05	Purchases		10	600	480	120			
08/05	College Crayons Ltd		6	23,140			23,140	27/05	ESB		11	350				350	
22/05	Sales		7	7,600	6,160	1,440		28/05	Wages		12	12,000					12,000
30/05	Jones Ltd		8	6,130			6,130	31/05	Ceres Ltd		13	1,450			1,450		
								31/05	Balance	c/d		18,150					
				44,450	11,160	2,440	29,270					44,450	480	120	1,450	350	24,000
01/06	Balance			18,150													

Cash and Bank Columns

Occasionally a business may use both a cash and bank column. In this case, a *contra* entry may arise.

1 Cash is lodged to the bank
2 Money is withdrawn from the bank and is held as cash in the office

Note that most of the opening and closing balances are included in the bank column (and cash column if you have one) in Method 2.

All the other entries are the same, no matter which method you use.

Tip

The bank column is part of the double-entry system.

Your revision notes

CHAPTER 28
Petty Cash Book

●●●**Learning Objectives**

Learn how to:

● enter figures from source documents
● balance the Petty Cash Book

Understand:

● Petty Cashier, Petty Cash Voucher
● Imprest system

Tip

Tick each one off when you feel confident that you know it.

The Petty Cash Book records small cash payments. It is usually used for small office expenses such as stamps and newspapers.

 **Understand**

The Imprest System

The Petty Cash Book works on the Imprest System, which works like this:

1   The Chief Cashier gives the Petty Cashier a sum of money known as the float or imprest. It is entered on the debit side of the Petty Cash Book.
2   This money is used to pay for small expenses during the month. A Petty Cash Voucher is filled in by the person spending the money. This is also signed by the manager authorising payment.
3   Payments are recorded on the credit side.
4   At the end of the month, the Petty Cash Book is balanced to find the total amount spent.
5   The Chief Cashier gives the Petty Cashier this amount of money (i.e. the amount spent). This brings the imprest/float back to what it was at the beginning of the month.

How to

Sample Question

(from H '00 II 6c)

Complete and balance the Petty Cash Book of a business for the month of May 2000 from the data below. Analyse the payments under the following headings: Postage; Cleaning; Travel; Stationery; Tea Break.

2000		Voucher No	IR£
1/5	Received a cheque for imprest		75.00
2/5	Purchased postage stamps	1	9.00
4/5	Paid for biscuits and milk	2	0.50
6/5	Paid for office cleaning	3	12.00
8/5	Purchased stapler and staples	4	9.50
12/5	Paid for taxi	5	7.50
14/5	Paid window cleaner	6	5.00
16/5	Paid for COD Parcel	7	6.50
19/5	Paid milk bill	8	3.50
23/5	Paid for bus fare	9	10.50
28/5	Received a cheque to restore the imprest		

Your revision notes

Answer

Solution

Date	Details	Fo	Total	Date	Details	Voucher No	Total	Postage	Cleaning	Travel	Stationery	Tea Break
01/05	Bank		75.00	02/05	Stamps	1	9.00	9.00				
				04/05	Biscuit, milk	2	0.50					0.50
				06/05	Office Cleaning	3	12.00		12.00			
				08/05	Stapler, Staples	4	9.50				9.50	
				12/05	Taxi	5	7.50			7.50		
				14/05	Window Cleaner	6	5.00		5.00			
				16/05	COD Parcel	7	6.50	6.50				
				19/05	Milk	8	3.50					3.50
				23/05	Bus Fare	9	10.50			10.50		3.50
			75.00				64.00	15.50	17.00	18.00	9.50	4.00
				21/05	Balance		11.00	GL/1	GL/2	GL/3	GL/4	GL/5
							75.00					
28/05	Balance		11.00									
	Bank		64.00									

Amount remaining at the end of the month

Total spent

The amount given by the Chief Cashier to restore the imprest

Tip

Note the difference in how the Petty Cash Book is balanced. Marks may be lost if it is balanced like the Analysed Cash Book.

Questions

Try these other questions

H '96 I B 3

The Ahalana Golf Club, in addition to using a cheque book, also makes cash payments for small amounts. These cash payments are authorised by the office manageress, Orla O'Sullivan, and recorded in the Petty Cash Book. The following cash transactions occurred in the month of April.

April	01	Received imprest for the month	€200 cheque
	04	Bought typing paper (Voucher 21)	€27
	06	Bought postage stamps (Voucher 22)	€10
	07	Refunded office assistant the price of office groceries (Voucher 23)	€3
	09	Gave donation to charity (Voucher 24)	€5
	12	Bought cleaning materials (Voucher 25)	€6
	14	Paid for registered letter (Voucher 26)	€3
	18	Paid cleaners' wages (Voucher 27)	€25
	23	Purchased computer paper (Voucher 28)	€15
	26	Paid for parcel post (Voucher 29)	€3

Complete and balance the Petty Cash Book for the month of April, using the following analysis columns; Postage, Stationery, Cleaning, Other expenses

H '03 I B 3(a)

●●●**Learning Objectives**

Learn how to:

- show how to record the writing-off of bad debts
- show purchases and sales of fixed assets
- enter opening and closing balances

Understand:

- transactions to record in General Journal
- the Accounting Equation

> **Tip**
>
> Tick each one off when you feel confident that you know it.

 **Understand**

The General Journal shows:

1   Opening and closing balances (i.e. The Trial Balance)
2   All credit transactions not involving goods purchased for resale, i.e.
    (a)   Purchases of fixed asset on credit
    (b)   Sale/disposal of fixed asset on credit
    (c)   Bad debt written off

> **Tip**
>
> Because many different types of transaction may be recorded in the General Journal, you need to include a short description of what happened. This is called the narration.

The Accounting Equation

Money invested by the owners of a company is called capital.

Assets are things the company owns.

Liabilities are money owed by the company.

Assets − Liabilities = Capital

 **How to**

Sample Question

H '99 II 1a

The books of Fergo Ltd showed the following opening and closing balances on 1 May 1999.

Machinery	€80,000
Creditor: Irwin Ltd	€22,000

Enter these balances in the General Journal and find the Ordinary Share Capital balance.

Solution

General Journal				
Date	Details	Fo.	Debit €	Credit €
May 01	Machinery		80,000	
	Creditor: Irwin Ltd			22,000
	Ordinary Share Capital			58,000
	(Being the Assets, Liabilities and Ordinary Share Capital)		80,000	80,000

Tip

The General Journal is kept in Record Book 2.

When entering the transaction in the General Journal, it is normal to make the debit entries first, then the credit entries.

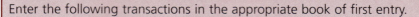

Sample Question

Enter the following transactions in the appropriate book of first entry.

24 June   St. Paul's Ink Ltd purchased a delivery van on credit from Ca Van Ltd for €20,000 + 20% VAT

16 July   Sold office furniture on credit to O'Riain Ltd for €3,000 + VAT at 20%

Solution

General Journal				
Date	Details	Fo.	Debit €	Credit €
June 01	Motor Vehicles	GL/1	20,000	
	VAT	GL/2	4,000	
	Ca Van Ltd	CL/1		24,000
	(Purchase of delivery van on credit)		24,000	24,000
July 16	O'Riain Ltd	DL/1	3,600	
	Office furniture	GL/3		3,000
	VAT	GL/2		600
	(Being the sale of office equipment on credit)		3,600	3,600

Your revision notes

Understand

Bad Debts

A bad debt is a debt you know you will not be repaid, usually because the debtor is bankrupt. Sometimes a debtor may pay part of the debt. This is usually written as X cent in the Euro. (e.g. 30c in the €).

How to

Sample Question

H '95 II 4 d(ii)

On 1 March 1995, Nikpan Ltd sold goods on credit to Elbat Ltd for €6,000 plus 12% VAT.

On 31 March 1995, Elbat Ltd informed Nikpan Ltd that it had gone bankrupt and could only pay 30c in the € and sent a cheque for this amount to Nikpan Ltd.

Nikpan Ltd then wrote off Elbat Ltd as a bad debt for the amount still due. Record the transaction in the General Journal.

Solution

Workings

€6,000 + 12%VAT =   €6,750 total
30c in the €   − €2,025 paid
                      €4,725 unpaid

General Journal				
Date	Details	Fo.	Debit	Credit
March 01	Bank	CB/1	2,025	
	Bad Debts	GL/4	4,725	
	Elbat Ltd	DL/1		6,750
	(Elbat Ltd declared bankrupt and paid 30c in the €. The balance written off as bad debt)			

Questions

Try these other questions

1   The books of Banba Ltd showed the following opening and closing balances on 1 May 2008.

Motor Vehicles	€45,000
Creditor: Shelly Ltd	€12,300
Debtor: Sham Blz Ltd	€6,700

Enter these balances in the General Journal and find the Ordinary Share Capital balance.

2   Enter the following transactions in the appropriate Book of First Entry.

24 March	Eiriú Ltd purchased Machinery on credit from Kennedy Ltd for €30,000 + 13% VAT
16 September	Sold office furniture on credit to Quinn Ltd for €3,000 + VAT at 20%

3   On 1 November 2009, Courtmacsherry Ltd sold goods on credit to Tory Ltd for €6,000 plus 21% VAT

On 31 November 2009, Tory Ltd informed Courtmacsherry Ltd that it had gone bankrupt and could only pay 25c in the € and sent a cheque for this amount to Courtmacsherry Ltd.

Courtmacsherry Ltd then wrote off Tory Ltd as a bad debt for the amount still due. Record the transaction in the General Journal.

H' 06 I A15

Your revision notes

CHAPTER 30
The Double Entry System & Integrated Questions

●●●**Learning Objectives**

Learn how to:

- post from books of first entry to ledger accounts
- complete 'integrated' questions
- complete paper II, question 1
- do prepayments and accruals

Understand:

- debit receiving account
- credit giving account
- asset, liability, expense, revenue
- use full date including year
- details column gives the name of the matching account
- folio column gives the source of the information

Tip

Tick each one off when you feel confident that you know it.

 **Understand**

Double-Entry System

The main accounts of a business are the ledger accounts.

The Books of First Entry (*Chapters 26–29*) summarise the main points of the source documents (*Chapter 25*) (i.e. What? How much? Who?)

Each asset, liability, expense and revenue has its own account. These accounts are kept in a ledger (a big book) or, more commonly today, in a computer. The ledger is normally divided into three parts:

The *Creditors' Ledger* (CL) has a separate account for each creditor. (A creditor is a business we owe money to. A creditor is a liability.)

The *Debtors' Ledger* (DL) has a separate account for each debtor. (A debtor is a business that owes money to us. A debtor is an asset.)

The *General Ledger* (GL) holds all other accounts.

Sample Question

H '01 I A 13

Complete the chart below, which traces the recording of business transactions through a firm's books and accounts, by writing the appropriate stages in the blank spaces at A and B.

Solution

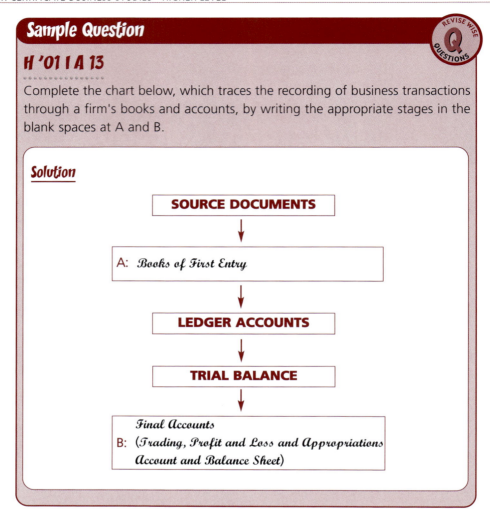

```
              ┌────────────────────────────┐
              │      SOURCE DOCUMENTS       │
              └────────────────────────────┘
                            │
                            ▼
┌──────────────────────────────────────────────────┐
│  A:   Books of First Entry                          │
└──────────────────────────────────────────────────┘
                            │
                            ▼
              ┌────────────────────────────┐
              │      LEDGER ACCOUNTS        │
              └────────────────────────────┘
                            │
                            ▼
              ┌────────────────────────────┐
              │      TRIAL BALANCE          │
              └────────────────────────────┘
                            │
                            ▼
┌──────────────────────────────────────────────────┐
│        Final Accounts                               │
│  B:   (Trading, Profit and Loss and Appropriations │
│        Account and Balance Sheet)                   │
└──────────────────────────────────────────────────┘
```

Tip

A very common type of question in Paper I, section A gives a transaction and asks you to name the accounts and say if the account is to be debited or credited.

The accounting system we use is called the Double-Entry System because each € is entered twice, once on the debit side and once on the credit side.

Debit the *Receiving* account   **Credit** the *Giving* account

Another way of looking at this is:

Asset = Something a business owns, or money owed to it (i.e. debtors). Assets usually have a debit balance.

DEBIT to record an increase in the value of an asset (e.g. debit machinery account for the purchase of machinery)	**CREDIT** to record a reduction on the value of an asset (e.g. credit the Jones Ltd account if debtor Jones Ltd makes a payment)

Liability = Money owed by a business (e.g. creditors, share capital). Liabilities have a credit balance.

DEBIT to record an reduction in the value of a liability (e.g. Debit Kinsella Ltd account if you make a payment to Creditor Kinsella Ltd)	**CREDIT** to record an increase in the value of a liability (e.g. debit the ordinary share capital account if shareholders invest more money in the company)

Expense = Something a business pays for (e.g. light and heat, purchases). An expense *prepaid* is an asset. An expense *due* is a liability.

DEBIT to record an increase in the value of an expense (e.g. debit purchases account for the purchase of goods for resale)	**CREDIT** to record a reduction in the value of an expense (e.g. credit the purchases returns account if you return goods purchased for resale)

Revenue = also called gain. Money earned by the business (e.g. sales, rent receivable) A revenue *prepaid* is a liability. A revenue *due* is an asset.

DEBIT to record a reduction in the value of a revenue (e.g. debit the sales returns account if goods sold by you are returned by a customer)	**CREDIT** to record an increase in the value of a revenue (e.g. debit the sales account if goods are sold)

How to

Sample Question

H '95 I A 14

Show how the following transaction would be recorded in the ledger of John O'Riordan, a retail grocer:

John O'Riordan bought new equipment on credit from McAuliffe Ltd for €2,500.

Solution

Debit Equipment **account**
Credit McAuliffe Ltd **account**

Tip

What was bought or sold?
   If an asset was bought, this is the receiving account ⇒ Debit
   If an asset was sold, this is the receiving account ⇒ Credit
If it involves goods for resale ⇒ Debit Purchases, Credit Sales
How was it paid for, cash or credit?
   Cash ⇒ the other account will be the bank account
   Credit ⇒ the other account will be the other business named in the question.
Remember, if you debit one account, you will credit another.

Sample Questions

H '97 I A 8

Show how the following transaction would be recorded in the ledger of Abbey Motors, a garage.
Abbey Motors bought cars for resale on credit from Car Importers Ltd.

Solution

Debit Purchases **account**
Credit Car Importers Ltd **account**

H '99 I A 9

Show how the following transaction would be recorded in the ledger of Computec Ltd, a computer manufacturing company.

Computec Ltd sold on credit a new computer to H. Maher.

Solution

Debit **H. Maher** account
Credit **Sales** account

H '05 I A 7

Complete the ledger accounts of Ryan's Garage, showing the names of the accounts and the relevant details.

On 17 August 2004, Ryan's Garage sells a car for €10,000 cash.

Date	Details	fo	€	Date	Details	fo	€
2004							
Aug 17			10,000				

Date	Details	fo	€	Date	Details	fo	€
				2004			
				Aug 17			10,000

Tip

The question has been rephrased, but you are still being asked what account to debit, and what to credit.

REVISE WISE TIP

Solution

Bank Account							
Date	Details	fo	€	Date	Details	fo	€
2004							
Aug 17	*Sales*	*SB/1*	10,000				

Sales Account							
Date	Details	fo	€	Date	Details	fo	€
				2004			
				Aug 17	*Bank*	*SB/1*	10,000

Tip

The 'Details' column shows the name of the other account in the double entry.

REVISE WISE TIP

Posting to the Ledgers

The process of taking information from the Books of First Entry and writing it in the ledger is called posting.

Purchasing is an expense to the business. The example below shows how details from the Purchases Day Book are posted to the ledger.

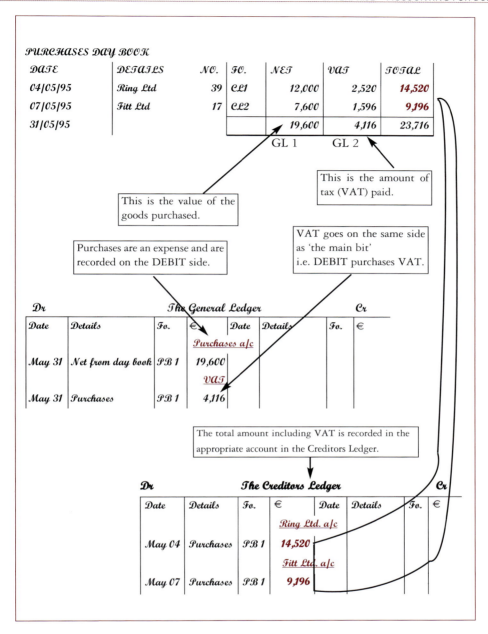

PURCHASES DAY BOOK

DATE	DETAILS	NO.	FO.	NET	VAT	TOTAL
04/05/95	Ring Ltd	39	CL1	12,000	2,520	14,520
07/05/95	Fitt Ltd	17	CL2	7,600	1,596	9,196
31/05/95				19,600	4,116	23,716
				GL 1	GL 2	

This is the value of the goods purchased.

This is the amount of tax (VAT) paid.

Purchases are an expense and are recorded on the DEBIT side.

VAT goes on the same side as 'the main bit' i.e. DEBIT purchases VAT.

The General Ledger

Dr					Cr			
Date	Details	Fo.	€	Date	Details	Fo.	€
			Purchases a/c				
May 31	Net from day book	PB 1	19,600				
			VAT				
May 31	Purchases	PB 1	4,116				

The total amount including VAT is recorded in the appropriate account in the Creditors Ledger.

The Creditors Ledger

Dr					Cr			
Date	Details	Fo.	€	Date	Details	Fo.	€
			Ring Ltd. a/c				
May 04	Purchases	PB 1	14,520				
			Fitt Ltd. a/c				
May 07	Purchases	PB 1	9,196				

Tip

There is only one VAT account.

There will be only one account in the debtors' ledger or creditors' ledger for any particular company.

REVISE WISE TIP

The other transactions are posted in a similar way:

Purchase (of goods for resale)

DEBIT	IN	CREDIT	IN
Purchases a/c		Creditor a/c	
VAT a/c		(The company	
	General Ledger	you bought from)	Creditors' Ledger

Sale (of goods)

DEBIT	IN	CREDIT	IN
Debtor a/c		Sales a/c	
(The company you		VAT a/c	
sold to)	Debtors' Ledger		General Ledger

Purchase Return (Returns Out)

DEBIT	IN	CREDIT	IN
Creditor a/c		Purchases Returns a/c	
(The company		VAT a/c	
you bought from)	Creditors' Ledger		General Ledger

Sales Return (Returns In)

DEBIT	IN	CREDIT	IN
Sales Returns a/c		Debtor a/c	
VAT a/c		(The company you	
	General Ledger	sold to)	Debtors' Ledger

Issuing Share Capital

DEBIT	IN	CREDIT	IN
Bank a/c	General Ledger (or Cash Book)	Ordinary Share Capital a/c	General Ledger

Borrowing Money

DEBIT	IN	CREDIT	IN
Bank a/c	General Ledger (or Cash Book)	Bank Loan a/c	General Ledger

Pay an Expense (e.g. Wages)

DEBIT	IN	CREDIT	IN
Wages a/c	General Ledger	Bank a/c	General Ledger (or Cash Book)

Purchase a Fixed Asset by Cheque (e.g. Machinery)

DEBIT	IN	CREDIT	IN
Machinery a/c	General Ledger	Bank a/c	General Ledger (or Cash Book)

Purchase a Fixed Asset on Credit (e.g. Machinery)

DEBIT	IN	CREDIT	IN
Machinery a/c	General Ledger	Creditor a/c (The company you bought from)	Creditors' Ledger

Sale of a Fixed Asset for cash (e.g. Machinery)

DEBIT	IN	CREDIT	IN
Bank a/c	General Ledger (or Cash Book)	Machinery a/c	General Ledger

Depreciation of a Fixed Asset (e.g. Motor Vehicle)

DEBIT	IN	CREDIT	IN
Profit and Loss a/c	General Ledger	Provision for Depreciation a/c	General Ledger

Receive a Gain (e.g. Rent Received)

DEBIT	IN	CREDIT	IN
Bank a/c	General Ledger (or Cash Book)	Rent Received a/c	General Ledger

Receive Payment from Debtor

DEBIT	IN	CREDIT	IN
Bank a/c	General Ledger (or Cash Book)	Debtor a/c	Debtors' Ledger

Make Payment to Creditor

DEBIT	IN	CREDIT	IN
Creditor a/c	Creditors' Ledger	Bank a/c	General Ledger (or Cash Book)

A Note on Integrated Questions

Many questions on paper II are titled 'This is an integrated…question', meaning that about 10–25 marks will be awarded for completing some bookkeeping task related to the question.

If you know the relationship between the different steps in the process:

Source document → Book of First Entry → Ledger → Trial Balance → Final Accounts

and can work out if an account is to be debited or credited, these are often straightforward questions.

Sample Question

H '96 II 5

d) On 1 January 1995, Jumbo Ltd purchased a delivery van by cheque for €26,000. Jumbo Ltd estimated that the delivery van would have a life of four years and an estimated scrap value of €2,000. Jumbo Ltd's trading year ends on 31 December 1995.

i) Record the purchase of the delivery van on 01/01/95 and the annual depreciation written off for the year ended 31/12/95 in the relevant accounts.

ii) Show the relevant entry in the balance sheet as on 31/12/95 (19 marks)

Depreciation

This question asks us to calculate the depreciation figure.

$$\frac{Cost - Scrap\ Value}{Life\ in\ Years} = \frac{€26,000 - €2,000}{4} = €6,000\ annual\ depreciation$$

Solution

Motor Vehicles a/c

Date	Details	fo	€	Date	Details	fo	€
1995							
Jan 1	Bank	GL 1	23,000				

Provision for Depreciation a/c

Date	Details	fo	€	Date	Details	fo	€
				1995			
				Dec 31	Profit + Loss a/c		6,000

Balance Sheet as at 31-12-95

Fixed Asset	Cost	Depreciation	NBV
Delivery Van	26,000	6,000	20,000

Understanding Accounts

Sometimes a question will ask you to explain the entries in an account. To do this you need to remember that the balance on an account will be either an asset or a liability.

	DR	CR
Expense	Prepaid = Asset	Due = Liability
Revenue	Due = Asset	Prepaid = Liability

Sample Question

REVISE WISE
Q
QUESTIONS

Explain the entries in the rent account below.

Rent Account

Date	Details	fo	€	Date	Details	fo	€
2008				2008			
Jan 1	Balance	b/d	300	Dec 31	P + L		1,440
Mar 1	Bank	CB1	1,080				
	Balance	c/d	60				
			1,380				1,380
					Balance	b/d	60

Solution

On 1 January 2008, St. Paul's Ink Ltd had a prepayment of €300 on their rent. They had paid in advance.
On 1 March, they paid €1,080 by cheque for rent.
On 31 December, €1,440 was transferred to the profit and loss account as the correct figure for the expense of rent for the year.
On 1 January 2009, they owed €60 in rent for the previous year.

Transferring to the Profit and Loss Account

Sometimes called closing off the accounts, this is when the balances are calculated at the end of the year with the expenses and gains transferred to the profit and loss account to calculate the profit or loss for the year.

Sample Question

H '95 I A 13

A firm has €80 insurance prepaid at the end of their financial year, 31 December 1994.

Balance the insurance account showing the amount transferred to the profit and loss account on 31 December 1994.

Insurance a/c

Date	Details	fo	€	Date	Details	fo	€
01-01-94	Balance	b/d	60				
01-03-94	Bank	GL4	480				

Tip

Insurance is an expense. The debit balance on 01/01/94 is an asset, i.e. insurance prepaid.

Solution

First write into the account everything you *do* know, and then work out the rest!

1. An expense will be on the debit side of the profit and loss account. That means 'profit and loss' will be on the credit side of the account, with a date at the end of the financial year
2. Lay out the account to balance. Leave at least two blank lines above the total for the moment
3. The balance prepaid on 31/12/94 will be brought down (b/d) on the debit side. That means it must be carried down (c/d) from the credit side
4. Total the debit side
5. This total is also the total for the credit side
6. The figure to transfer to the profit and loss account for the year is the total less the balance c/d

Light and Heat a/c

01-01-94	Balance	b/d	60	31-12-94	Profit & Loss		460
01-03-94	Bank	GL4	480				
				31-12-94	Balance	c/d	80
			540				540
31-12-94	Balance	b/d	80				

Paper II Question 1

Of all the questions on paper II this is the question fewest students attempt, but there is no reason to be afraid of it. The main problem with the question is time, but with practice you will learn to work quickly.

The question generally asks you to do four things:

1 **General Journal** Record information in the general journal and then post the correct figures to the appropriate ledger accounts
2 **Books of First Entry** (Purchases/Purchases Returns/Sales/Sales Returns Day Book) Post the information from the Books of First Entry to the appropriate ledger accounts
3 **Record cash/bank transactions** in the analysed receipts and lodgements and analysed cash and cheque payments book (or analysed cash book)
4 **Balance** the ledger accounts and extract a trial balance.

Note that the questions are usually written assuming you will answer with an analysed cash book, but you may answer using either the modern or traditional layout.

Sample Question

H '01 II 1

THAEM Ltd had the following balances in its general journal on 1 May 2001:

General Journal

Date	Details	fo.	Debit	Credit
01-05-01	Buildings	GL1	120,000	
	Debtor SAM Ltd	DL1	56,000	
	Bank Overdraft	CB1		25,000
	Ordinary Share Capital	GL2		151,000
	(Being the Assets, Liabilities and Share Capital of THAEM Ltd)		176,000	176,000

a) Post the balances in the above general journal to the relevant ledger accounts. (5 marks)
b) Post the relevant figures from the Sales and Purchases books below to the ledgers.

Sales Book (Page 1)

Date	Details	invoice	fo	Net	VAT	Total
07-05-01	MA Ltd	53	DL2	24,000	3,000	27,000
				GL3	GL4	

Purchases Book (Page 1)

Date	Details	invoice	fo	Net	VAT	Total
09-05-01	GUIRE Ltd	12	CL2	32,000	4,000	36,000
				GL5	GL4	

(7 marks)

c) Record the following bank transactions for the month of May. Post relevant figures to the ledger.

Note: Analyse the bank transactions using the following money column headings:

Debit (Receipts) Side: Bank; Sales; VAT; Debtors
Credit (Payments) Side: Bank; Purchases; VAT; Creditors; Insurance

03-05-01	Cash sales lodged		€54,000 (€48,000 + €6,000 VAT)
04-05-01	Purchases for resale	Cheque 1	€30,000 + VAT 12½%
13-05-01	SAM Ltd paid its account in full and this was lodged		Receipt 43
19-05-01	Paid GUIRE Ltd	Cheque 2	€26,000
24-05-01	MA Ltd paid €7,000 and this was lodged		Receipt 44
28-05-01	Paid for insurance	Cheque 3	€4,600

(19 marks)

d) Balance the accounts on 31 May 2001 and extract a trial balance as at that date. (9 marks)

Solution

Dr.   **Cr**

Date 2001	Details	Fo.	€	Date 2001	Details	Fo.	€
			General Ledger				
			Buildings a/c (p.1)				
02-May	Balance	GJ	120,000				
			Ordinary Share Capital a/c				
				02-May	Balance	GJ	151,000
			Insurance a/c (p.3)				
29-May	Bank	CB	4,600				
			Sales a/c (p.4)				
				01-Jun	Total Debtors	SDB	24,000
					Bank	CB	48,000
							72,000
			Purchases a/c (p.5)				
01-Jun	Total Creditors	PDB	32,000				
	Bank	CB	30,000				
			62,000				
			VAT a/c (p.6)				
01-Jun	Credit Purchases	PDB	4,000	01-Jun	Credit Sales	SDB	3,000
	Cash Purchases	CB	3,750		Cash Sales	CB	6,000
	Balance	c/d	1,250				
			9,000				9,000
				02-Jun	Balance	b/d	1,250
			Debtors Ledger (Sales Ledger)				
			SAM Ltd. a/c (p.1)				
02-May	Balance	GJ	56,000	14-May	Bank	CB	56,000
			MA Ltd. a/c (p.2)				
08-May	Sales	SDB	27,000	25-May	Bank	CB	7,000
				01-Jun	Balance	c/d	20,000
			27,000				27,000
02-Jun	Balance	b/d	20,000				
			Creditors Ledger (Purchases Ledger)				
			Guire Ltd. a/c (p.1)				
20-May	Bank	CB	26,000	10-May	Purchases	PDB	36,000
01-Jun	Balance	c/d	10,000				
			36,000				36,000
				02-Jun	Balance	b/d	10,000

ANALYSED CASH BOOK (Debit Side)

Date	Details	no.	Fo.	Bank	Sales	VAT	Debtors
2001							
04-May	Sales		GL4	54,000	48,000	6,000	
14-May	SAM Ltd.	43	DL1	56,000			56,000
25-May	MA Ltd.	44	DL2	7,000			7,000
			①	117,000	48,000	6,000	63,000
02-Jun	Balance		b/d	27,650			

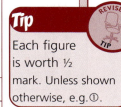

Tip

Each figure is worth ½ mark. Unless shown otherwise, e.g.①.

ANALYSED CASH BOOK (Credit Side)

Date	Details	no.	Fo.	Bank	Purchases	VAT	Creditors	Insurance
2001								
02-May	Balance		b/d	① 25,000				
05-May	Purchases	1	GL5	33,750	30,000	3,750		
20-May	GUIRE Ltd.	2	CL1	26,000			26,000	
29-May	Insurance	3		4,600				4,600
02-Jun	Balance		c/d	27,650	①			
				117,000	30,000	3,750	26,000	4,600

Trial Balance as on 31-5-01

	Dr.	Cr.
Bank	27,650	
Buildings	120,000	
MA Ltd.	20,000	
Insurance	4,600	
Purchases	62,000	
Ordinary Share Capital		151,000
GUIRE Ltd.		10,000
Sales		72,000
VAT		1,250
	234,250	234,250

Tip

The mark is given for using figures from your own ledgers.

Tip

- The year needs to be in the date column at least once.
- The Fo. Column in the ledger shows which book of first entry the information came from
- Each ledger entry is worth 1 mark.
- Each balance is worth 1 mark.
- Make sure you include the year in the date
- Marks will be lost if the folio (Fo.) column is incomplete.

Questions

Try these other questions

H '97 I A 6

Select the correct word from the following list and write it in the space provided to complete the statement below.

| debit | no | credit |

a) Assets have _____ balances in their accounts.
b) Liabilities have _____ balances in their accounts.

H '96 I A 13

In the space provided, name the two accounts affected by the following transaction in the ledger of Mary Kelly, a retail grocer.
Mary Kelly sold equipment on credit to Gromore Ltd for €3,000.

Debit _____ account
Credit _____ account

H '98 I A 12

Show how the following transaction would be recorded in the ledger of Castle Carriers, a courier service company.

Castle Carriers bought a new motor van on credit from Transo Ltd.

Debit _____ account
Credit _____ account

H '00 I A 16

Show how the following transaction would be recorded in the ledger of Tom O'Shea, a retail draper.

Tom O'Shea purchased new equipment on credit from Quick Fix Ltd for €15,000.

Debit _____ account

Credit _____ account

More of this type of question

H '01 I A 6   **H '03 I A 19**

H '04 I A 11

Questions

H '96 I A 5

The following is an extract from a profit and loss account of a firm for the year ending 31/12/1995.

Insurance	560	
Less insurance prepaid	160	
		400

a) What was the figure for insurance used during the year?

Answer_____

b) What was the figure for insurance paid during the year?

Answer_____

H'97 I A 4

The following account appeared in the ledger of Hidro Ltd:

Wages a/c

24-12-96	Bank	C.B9	300	31/12/96	Profit & Loss	GL	400
31-12-96	Balance	c/d	100				
			400				400
				31-12-96	Balance	b/d	100

Indicate, by means of a tick (✓), the correct answer to the following.

a) Does the above account have a debit or credit balance?

Debit ☐

Credit ☐

b) What does the balance in this account mean?

H '99 I A 16

A firm owed €150 for Light and Heat on 31/12/98.

Balance the Light and Heat account below showing the amount transferred to the final accounts on the 31/12/98.

Light and Heat a/c

Date	Details	F	€	Date	Details	F	€
20-9-98	Bank	C.B.	630				

More of this type of question

H '06 I A 20

H '04 I A 16   H '04 I A 20

H '03 I A 11   H '03 I A 12

H '02 I A 13   H '01 I A 8

H '01 I A 18

Questions

Integrated Questions

H '06 II 5(D)

H '05 II 2(B,C)   H '05 II 5(B)

H '04 II 2(C)   H '03 II 2(C)

H '03 II 5(D)   H '02 II 3(BII)

H '02 II 5(D)   H '01 II 2(D)

Questions

Long Questions

H '06 II 1

H '05 II 1   H '04 II 1

H '03 II 1   H '02 II 1

H '01 II 1   H '00 II 1

REVISE WISE QUESTIONS

Your revision notes

●●●**Learning Objectives**

Learn how to:

- prepare a creditors' control account
- prepare a debtors' control account

Understand:

- creditors' control account
- debtors' control account

> **Tip**
>
> Tick each one off when you feel confident that you know it.

 **Understand**

The debtors' control account checks the accuracy of the debtors' (sales) ledger.

The creditors' control account checks the accuracy of the creditors' (purchases) ledger.

Control accounts are not part of the double-entry system.

> **Tip**
>
> Any figure on the debit side of an account will be on the debit side of the control account.
>
> Any figure on the credit side of an account will be on the credit side of the control account.

How to

Debtors' Control Account

1 Balance each account in the debtors' ledger
2 Total these balances
3 Open the debtors' control account
    i Debit the opening balances (from trial balance or general journal)
    ii Debit total credit sales (from Sales Day Book)
    iii Credit total sales returns (from Sales Return Day Book)
    iv Credit total payments received (from Cash Book)
    v Balance the debtors' control account
4 The control account balance should equal the total of the debtors' ledger balances

Sample Question

H'95 I A 3

Complete and balance the debtors' control account below from the following information:

1 May	Debtors' balance	€970
	Total credit sales for May	€10,350
	Total cash received from debtors	€9,780

Tip

Steps 1 and 2 are done for you in this question.

Solution

Debtors' Control Account

Date	Details		€	Date	Details		€
01/05	Balance b/d		970	31/05	Lodgements	CB	9,780
31/05	Credit Sales	SDB	10,350				
					Balance c/d		1,540
			11,320				11,320
01/06	Balance c/d		1,540				

Creditors' Control Account

1 Balance each account in the creditors' ledger
2 Total these balances
3 Open the debit control account
   i   Credit the opening balances (from trial balance or general journal)
   ii Credit total purchases (from Purchases Day Book)
   iii Debit total purchase returns (from Purchase Return Day Book)
   iv Debit total payments made (from cheques issued)
   v   Balance the creditors' control account
4 The control account balance should equal the total of the creditors' ledger balances

Sample Question

H'98 1 A 19

NB This question actually asked for the 'Continuous Balance', presentation but the T presentation is shown here.

Complete and balance the creditors' control account below for May from the following information:

Total purchases on credit in May	€12,600
Total payments (by cheque) during May to creditors	€11,500
Cash purchases during May	€1,260

The opening balance is €2,400.

Solution

Creditors' Control Account

Date	Details		€	Date	Details		€
31/05	Payments	CB	11,500	01/05	Balance b/d		2,400
				31/05	Credit Purchases	PDB	12,600
31/05	Balance c/d		3,500				
			15,000				15,000
				01/06	Balance c/d		3,500

Tip

Cash purchases are not used in the creditors' control account as they do not involve purchases on credit.

Questions

H'00 1 A 8

From the following information, complete and balance the debtors' control account below for the month of May:

Total credit sales for May	€35,764
Total cash received from debtors	€29,498
Total sales returns	€3,927

There was no opening balance.

H' 06 1 A 9

H' 05 1 A B

Your revision notes

CHAPTER 32
Continuous Presentation

●●●Learning Objectives

Learn how to:

- convert from T presentation to continuous balance presentation
- convert from continuous balance presentation to T presentation

Tip

Tick each one off when you feel confident you know it.

T Presentation

The account is shown with two sides: the debit side and credit side. At the end of the period (week, month or year), the account is balanced to find out how much is in it.

Continuous Balance Presentation

With the continuous balance format, the balance is recalculated after each transaction instead of once at the end.

How to

Converting from T Presentation to Continuous Balance Presentation

1 First decide if the account would usually have a debit balance (asset and expense) or a credit balance (liability and revenue/gain)
2 Any entry on the debit side of the T will go in the debit column of the continuous balance format. Any entry on the credit side will go on the credit column
3 If the account usually has a debit balance, add figures in the debit column and subtract those in the credit column
4 If the account usually has a credit balance, then add the credits and subtract the debits

Tip

All entries in the continuous balance are made in the order they happened.

Sample Question

H'96 I A8

The following account appeared in your creditors' ledger:

DR   D. Nolan a/c   CR

Date	Details	fo	€	Date	Details	fo	€
May 6	Bank	C.B.	580	May 1	Balance	b/d	460
				May 4	Purchases	P/B	370

Rewrite D. Nolan's account in the continuous balance form below.

Solution

	D. Nolan (Creditor) a/c					
Date	Details	fo	DR	CR	Balance	
May 1	Balance	b/d			460	This is a credit balance
May 4	Purchases	PB		370	830	Add the credit
May 6	Bank	CB	580		250	Subtract the debit

Sample Question

The following account appears in your debtor's ledger:

DR   D. Hurley a/c   CR

Date	Details	fo	€	Date	Details	fo	€
Aug 1	Balance	b/d	3,400	Aug 13	Bank	CB	12,200
Aug 9	Sales	SB	14,300				

Rewrite D. Hurley's account in the continuous balance form below:

Solution

D. Hurley (Debtor) a/c

Date	Details	fo	DR	CR	Balance	
Aug 1	Balance	b/d			3,400	This is a debit balance
Aug 9	Sales	SB	14,300		17,700	Add the debit
Aug 13	Bank	CB		12,200	5,500	Subtract the debit

Converting from Continuous Balance to T Presentation

1 Is the balance a debit balance or a credit balance? It may have a DR or CR beside it. Otherwise, what type of account is it? Remember, assets and expenses usually have a debit balance (a debtor is an asset); liabilities and revenues usually have a credit balance (a creditor is a liability)

2 Open the T account and enter the balance from the **first** line of the continuous balance account

3 Any figures from the debit column are entered in the debit side of the T account. Any figures for the credit column are entered in the credit side of the T account

4 Balance the account in the usual way

Sample Question

The following account appeared in the general ledger of St. Paul's Ink Ltd.

Bank Account					
Date	Details	fo	DR	CR	Balance
Jun 01	Balance	b/d			375cr
04	Sales	GL/2	1,450		1,075
09	Creditor (Lavelle)	CL/3		890	185
14	Machinery	GL/4		1,200	1,015cr
21	Ordinary Share Capital	GL/1	5,000		3,985

Rewrite the bank account in T-Presentation below.

Solution

Bank Account

Date	Details	fo	€	Date	Details	fo	€
Jun 04	Sales	GL/2	1,450	Jun 01	Balance	b/d	375
21	Ordinary Share Capital	GL/1	5,000	09	Creditor (Lavelle)	CL/3	890
				14	Machinery	GL/4	1,200
					Balance	c/d	3,985
			6,450				6,450
Jul 01	Balance	b/d	3,985				

Tip

The bank account is an asset, so it usually has a **debit** balance.
In this question you are told that the opening balance is a **credit** balance.

Question

Try this other question

H '02 I A 15

Final Accounts and Balance Sheet

●●●Learning Objectives

Learn how to:

- prepare the various accounts:
  - ○ trading account
  - ○ profit and loss account
  - ○ profit and loss appropriations account
  - ○ balance sheet

Understand:

- turnover
- gross profit, net profit
- gains (non-trading revenue), expenses
- dividend, retained profit/reserve
- capital employed

Tip

Tick each one off when you feel confident you know it.

How to

The final accounts show how the business has performed over time; i.e. did they make a profit or a loss and what assets and liabilities the company had on a certain date.

i. The Trading Account

$$
\begin{array}{l}
\text{Sales} \\
-\ \text{Cost of Sales} \\
\hline
=\ \text{Gross Profit}
\end{array}
$$

The Cost of Sales may include purchases, carriage in, direct manufacturing costs or import duties.

Sample Question

The following information was extracted from the books of Cameron Ltd on 31 May 2008.

You are required to prepare the company's trading account for the year ended 31 May 2008.

Purchases	96,000
Sales	204,000
Opening Stock	13,000
Carriage in	800
Sales Returns	2,000
Closing Stock	11,100

Solution

Trading Account of Cameron Ltd for the Year Ended 31-05-08

Sales			204,000
Less Sales Returns			2,000
			202,000
Less Cost of Sales			
Opening Stock		13,000	
Purchases	96,000		
Carriage in	800	96,800	
Cost of goods available		109,800	
Closing Stock		11,100	
Cost Of Goods Sold			98,700
Gross Profit			103,300

Tip

Marks may be lost if you do not put a title on the account showing the name of the company and the time period covered.

Turnover = Sales – Sales Returns

If presented with a trading account with a missing figure, you must be able to work out what is missing.

Sample Question

H '97 I A 19

Trading A/C for year ending 31/12/93.

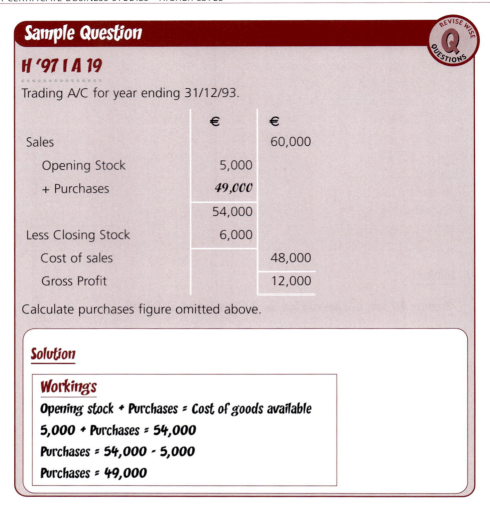

	€	€
Sales		60,000
Opening Stock	5,000	
+ Purchases	49,000	
	54,000	
Less Closing Stock	6,000	
Cost of sales		48,000
Gross Profit		12,000

Calculate purchases figure omitted above.

Solution

Workings
Opening stock + Purchases = Cost of goods available

5,000 + Purchases = 54,000

Purchases = 54,000 - 5,000

Purchases = 49,000

ii. Profit and Loss Account

This account follows directly from the trading account. It starts with the gross profit and adds any other income (gains) before subtracting all other expenses.

Gains
 i) Any non-trading income
 ii) Bad debts recovered are shown as gains

Expenses
The day-to-day costs involved in running the business (wages, insurance etc.).

Sample Question

The following balances were extracted from the books of Dowling Ltd on 30 April 2009.

You are required to prepare the company's profit and loss account for the year ended 30 April 2009.

	€
Gross Profit	95,050
Wages	31,000
Loan Interest	1,400
Commission Receivable	6,000
Depreciation	10,400
Rent	5,600

Solution

Profit and Loss Account of Dowling Ltd for the Year Ended 30-04-09

Gross Profit		95,050
add Gains		
Commission Receivable		6,000
		101,050
less Expenses		
Wages	31,000	
Loan interest	1,400	
Depreciation	10,400	
Rent	5,600	
		48,400
Net Profit		52,650

Tip

Anything with the word 'received' or 'receivable' is a gain.
Only current expenditure goes in expenses.

iii. Profit and Loss Appropriations Account

Follows directly from the profit and loss account.

A business can do two things with any profit it earns:

1 It can pay the profit to the shareholders who own the company. This is called a dividend

2 It can keep the profit in the business (retained earnings). This would be invested in the business, for example by buying new machinery or developing a new product.

Tip

Any dividend is always calculates as a percentage (%) of Issued Share Capital.

Sample Question

You are given the following information about Nelson Ltd for the year ended 31-12-08:

Sales	€460,000
Net Profit	€28,000
Issued Share Capital	€120,000
Dividend Paid	15%

Calculate the dividend paid and prepare the profit and loss appropriation account.

Solution

Dividend Paid = 15% of issued share capital, i.e. €120,000 x 15% = €18,000

Tip

The balance of the profit (€10,000) is retained by the company for future investment.

Profit and Loss Appropriation Account of Nelson Ltd for the year ended 31-12-08

Net Profit			28,000
Ordinary Share Dividend			18,000
Retained Earnings			10,000

Tip

Retained earnings are also known as revenue reserves.

iv. The Balance Sheet

If the trading, profit and loss and appropriations accounts show what has happened in the course of a year, the balance sheet shows how things are right now.

The balance sheet is a list of all the company's assets and liabilities laid out in a standard format so it can be understood more easily.

The balance sheet is divided into four main sections.

Fixed Assets: Something the company owns which lasts a long time:
    Buildings
    Machinery
    Motor vehicles
    Equipment
    Fixtures and fittings

Current Assets: Something the company owns which is constantly changing:
    Stock
    Debtors
    Cash in bank
    Cash in hand

Current Liabilities: Money owed by the company payable within one year:
    Creditors
    Overdraft

Financed By:
    Share Capital
    Reserves
    Long-term liabilities

Sample Question

The following balances were extracted from the books of Rickard Ltd on 31 March 2009. The authorised share capital is 250,000 €1 ordinary shares. You are required to prepare the company's balance sheet as at 31 March 2009.

	€
Retained Earnings	25,460
Buildings	120,000
Machinery	45,000
Closing Stock	12,400
Debtors	6,570
Creditors	4,530
Cash in hand	850
Bank Overdraft	2,190
Issued Share Capital	100,000
Mortgage	53,000

Solution

Balance Sheet of Rickard Ltd as at 31 March 2009

Fixed Assets			
Buildings			120,000
Machinery			45,000
			165,000
Current Assets			
Closing Stock		12,400	
Debtors		6,750	
Cash in Hand		850	
		20,000	
Current Liabilities			
Creditors	4,350		
Bank Overdraft	2,190	6,540	
Working Capital			13,460
Total Net Assets			178,460
Financed By			
Share Capital			
Authorised			250,000
Issued			
100,000 €1 shares			100,000
Reserves			
Retained Earnings			25,460
Long Term Liabilities			
Mortgage			53,000
Capital Employed			178,460

Tip

Issued share capital plus reserves is known as shareholders' funds.

Sample Question

H '00 I A 11

The purchase of stock with the aid of a bank overdraft affects the balance sheet in one of the following ways:

a) Current assets increase and current liabilities decrease ☐
b) Current assets decrease and current liabilities decrease ☐
c) Current assets increase and current liabilities increase ☐
d) Current assets decrease and current liabilities increase ☐

Tip

To answer the question, read it carefully to make sure you understand what you are being asked to do.
1 Where does 'stock' go in the balance sheet? (*in current assets*)
2 And stock is increasing
3 Where does 'bank overdraft' go in the balance sheet? (*current liabilities*)
4 And there is a new Overdraft

Solution

c) Current assets increase and current liabilities increase ☑

Questions

Try these other questions

Trading a/c	Profit and Loss a/c	Appropriations a/c	Balance Sheet
H '06 I A 3(a)	H '01 I A 5	H '04 I A 18	H '06 I A 11
H '04 I A 3 b			H '04 I A 14
H '02 I A 17 a			H '00 I A 16
			H '01 I A 10 a

CHAPTER 34
Final Accounts with Adjustments

●●●**Learning Objectives**

Learn how to:

- make adjustments for prepayments/accruals, bad debts, dividend declared

Understand:

- add DUE
- subtract PREPAID
- dividend, retained profit/reserves

Tip

Tick each one off when you feel confident you know it.

REVISE WISE TIP

There has been a final accounts and balance sheet question on Paper II in the Junior Certificate exam every year. The question generally asks you to prepare a trading, profit and loss and appropriations account and a balance sheet from a trial balance with some additional information. This information will require you to make some adjustments to figures given in the trial balance before using it.

Understand

REVISE WISE UNDERSTANDING

The Adjustments

The profit and loss account should show all the expenses incurred and revenues earned during the year. It does not matter when the expense is actually paid or the revenue actually received; the important thing is when it was incurred.

1 Expense Due
An expense due is a current liability.

Sample Question

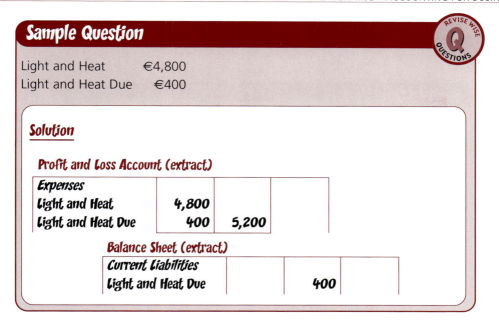

Light and Heat   €4,800
Light and Heat Due   €400

Solution

Profit and Loss Account (extract)

Expenses			
Light and Heat	4,800		
Light and Heat Due	400	5,200	

Balance Sheet (extract)

Current Liabilities			
Light and Heat Due		400	

2 Revenue Due

Revenue due is money earned by the company which it has yet to receive. It is a current asset.

Sample Question

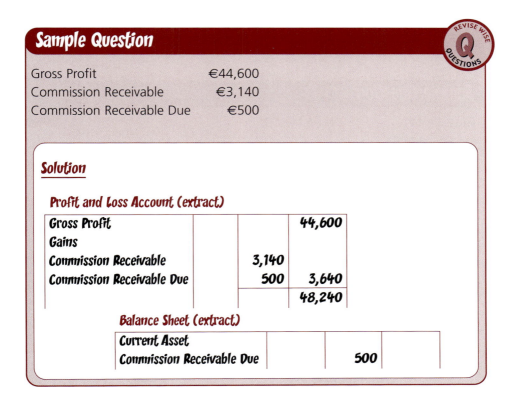

Gross Profit   €44,600
Commission Receivable   €3,140
Commission Receivable Due   €500

Solution

Profit and Loss Account (extract)

Gross Profit			44,600
Gains			
Commission Receivable		3,140	
Commission Receivable Due		500	3,640
			48,240

Balance Sheet (extract)

Current Asset			
Commission Receivable Due		500	

227

3 Expense Prepaid

An expense prepaid is when you pay for something in advance.

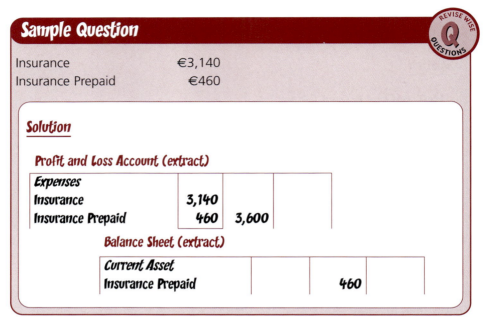

Sample Question

| Insurance | €3,140 |
| Insurance Prepaid | €460 |

Solution

Profit and Loss Account (extract)

Expenses			
Insurance	3,140		
Insurance Prepaid	460	3,600	

Balance Sheet (extract)

Current Asset			
Insurance Prepaid		460	

4 Revenue Prepaid

Revenue prepaid is where you have been paid for a service which you have yet to provide.

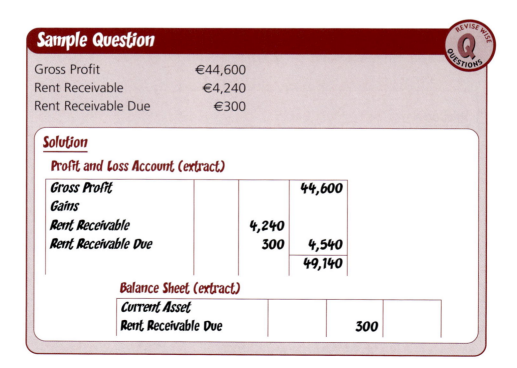

Sample Question

Gross Profit	€44,600
Rent Receivable	€4,240
Rent Receivable Due	€300

Solution

Profit and Loss Account (extract)

Gross Profit		44,600
Gains		
Rent Receivable	4,240	
Rent Receivable Due	300	4,540
		49,140

Balance Sheet (extract)

Current Asset			
Rent Receivable Due		300	

5 Depreciation

As fixed assets get older, they lose value due to wear and tear and usage. This loss of value is called depreciation.

Sample Question

| Buildings | €150,000 |
| Machinery | €45,000 |

| Depreciation: | Buildings | 5% per year |
| | Machinery | 20% per year |

Solution

Profit and Loss Account (extract)

Expenses		
Depreciation: Buildings	7,500	
Machinery	9,000	16,500

Balance Sheet (extract)

Fixed Assets	Cost	Depreciation	NBV
Buildings	150,000	7,500	142,500
Machinery	45,000	9,000	36,000
	195,000	16,500	178,500

Workings

Buildings
5% of €150,000 = €7,500
Machinery
20% of €45,000 = €9,000

Tip

NBV = Net Book Value (Cost – Depreciation).

6 Bad Debts

A bad debt is a sum owed to the business by a debtor that you are sure will not be paid (e.g. the debtor has been declared bankrupt).

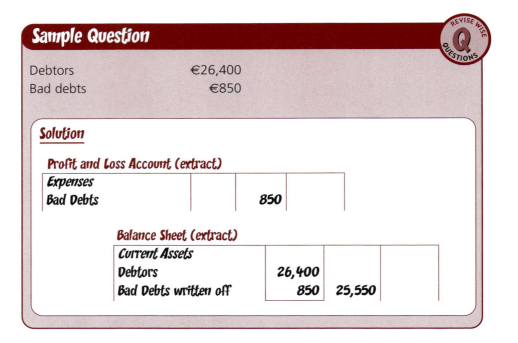

Sample Question

Debtors	€26,400
Bad debts	€850

Solution

Profit and Loss Account (extract)

Expenses			
Bad Debts		850	

Balance Sheet (extract)

Current Assets			
Debtors		26,400	
Bad Debts written off		850	25,550

Tip

If a figure for bad debts is included in the **trial balance**, it means that it has already been subtracted from debtors. In this case, you only need to include it with the other expenses.

7 Dividend Declared

A dividend declared is a dividend the company has said it will pay, but has yet to do so. It is a current liability until it is paid.

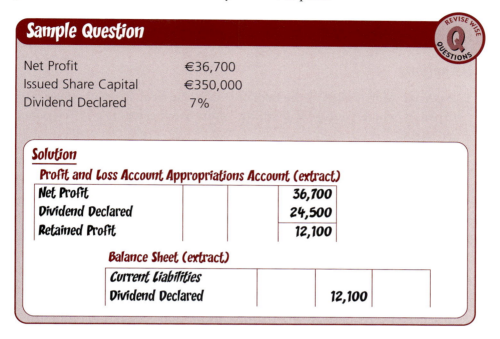

Sample Question

Net Profit	€36,700
Issued Share Capital	€350,000
Dividend Declared	7%

Solution

Profit and Loss Account Appropriations Account (extract)

Net Profit			36,700
Dividend Declared			24,500
Retained Profit			12,100

Balance Sheet (extract)

Current Liabilities			
Dividend Declared		12,100	

Adjustment	Example	Trading, Profit and Loss Account	Balance Sheet
Carriage in	Carriage in Due	Add to Carriage in	Current Liability
	Carriage in prepaid	Subtract from Carriage in	Current Asset
Accruals			
Expense Due	Wages Due	Add to Expense	Current Liability
Gain Due	Commission Receivable Due	Add to Gain	Current Asset
Prepayments			
Gain Prepaid	Interest Receivable Prepaid	Subtract from Gain	Current Liability
Expense Prepaid	Rent Prepaid	Subtract from Expense	Current Asset
Depreciation		an Expense	Subtract from Fixed Assets
Bad Debt		an Expense	Subtract from Debtors
Dividend Declared		Subtract from Net Profit	Current Liability

Tip

Carriage In is a part of the cost of goods and must be added to purchases.
Carriage Out is a cost of distribution and is shown in the profit and loss account.

Definitions

1 **Accrual**: Money *owed by* the firm or *owed to* the firm. They are most often expenses where you use something before paying for it, e.g. telephone, electricity
2 **Prepayment**: Money paid in advance

 **How to**

Reading the Question

The information is presented in two parts.
- **The Trial Balance**
  This lists the balances from each account. Every figure in the trial balance is used once in the trading, profit and loss and appropriations account or in the balance sheet
- **Additional Information**
  These are adjustments you need to make to the figures in the accounts

Tip

All figures given in 'Additional Information' will be used **twice**, once in the trading, profit and loss and appropriations account and once in the balance sheet.

Approaching the Question

1 Read through the trial balance and decide where each figure should be used. Put a letter with each item to remind you of this

T = Trading Account	FA = Fixed Assets
G = Gains (in the Profit and Loss Account)	CA = Current Assets
E = Expenses (in the Profit and Loss Account)	CL = Current Liabilities
A = Appropriations Account	FB = Financed By

2 Look at the Additional information. Put letters with it to show each place it should be used. Also mark with an asterisk (*) the trial balance item to be adjusted
3 Enter all the figures in the accounts
4 Tick each figure as you use it

Tip

Closing stock is always given with the adjustments and is used in the balance sheet as a current asset and also in the trading account.

Sample Question

The following trial balance was extracted from the books of COLVIN Ltd on 31 May 2008.

The Authorised Share Capital was 500,000 €1 ordinary shares.

Any date can be used for the end of the year. In this case it is 31/05/08.
This figure is needed for the balance sheet.

Trial Balance	Dr	Cr	
Purchases and Sales	T 250,000	T 560,000	
Returns In and Returns Out	T 4,800	T 3,200	
Debtors * and Creditors	CA 32,300	CL 27,600	
Wages and Salaries *	E 100,000		
Carriage Out	E 2,500		
Carriage In *	T 2,800		
Advertising *	E 23,050		
Rent Receivable *		G 8,400	
Interest Receivable *		G 400	
Buildings *	FA 480,000		
Machinery *	FA 110,000		
Opening Stock	T 21,850		
Issued Share Capital		FB 350,000	
Bank		CL 1,200	*NB This is a Bank Overdraft*
Long term Loan		FB 65,000	
Profit and Loss Balance		A 11,500	
	1,027,300	1,027,300	

You are required to prepare the company's **trading, profit and loss and appropriation accounts** for the year ended 31 May 2008 and a **balance sheet** as on that date.

You are given the following information as on 31 May 2008.

Carriage In Due	400	T	CL	
Closing Stock	25,000	T	CA	
Interest Receivable Due	150	G	CA	
Rent Receivable Prepaid	700	G	CL	
Wages and Salaries Due	2,500	E	CL	
Advertising Prepaid	4,050	E	CA	
Bad Debt	1,100	E	CL	
Depreciation: Buildings	2%	E	FA	
Machinery	10%	E	FA	
Dividend Declared	19,000	A	CL	

Solution

Trading, Profit & Loss and Appropriations Account of COLVIN Ltd for the year ended 31/12/08

Sales		560,000	
Sales Returns		4,800	555,200
less Cost Of Sales			
Opening Stock		21,850	
Purchases	250,000		
Purchases Returns	3,200		
		246,800	
Carriage In	2,800		
Carriage In Due	400	3,200	
Cost Of Goods Available		271,850	
Closing Stock		25,000	
Cost Of Goods Sold			246,850
GROSS PROFIT			308,350
add GAINS			
Interest Receivable		400	
Interest Receivable Due		150	550
Rent Receivable		8,400	
Rent Receivable Prepaid		700	1,700
			316,600

less EXPENSES			
Wages & Salaries	100,000		
Wages & Salaries Due	2,500	102,500	
Bad Debts		1,100	
Advertising	23,050		
Advertising Prepaid	4,050	19,000	
Carriage Out		2,500	
Depreciation:			
premises	9,600		
machinery	11,000	20,600	147,700
NET PROFIT			170,900
Profit and Loss Balance			11,500
			182,400
less Dividend Declared			19,000
RETAINED PROFIT			163,400

Your revision notes

Balance Sheet of COLVIN Ltd as at 31/12/08			
Fixed Assets	Cost	Depreciation	NBV
Premises	480,000	9,600	470,400
Machinery	110,000	11,000	99,000
	590,000	20,600	569,400
CURRENT ASSETS			
Closing Stock		25,000	
Debtors	32,300		
Bad Debts	1,100	31,200	
Interest Receivable Due		150	
Advertising Prepaid		4,050	
		60,400	
CURRENT LIABILITIES			
Creditors	27,600		
Overdraft	1,200		
Customs Duty Due	400		
Wages and Salaries Due	2,500		
Rent Receivable Prepaid	700		
Dividend Declared	19,000	51,400	
Working Capital			9,000
Net Total Assets			578,400
Authorised Share Capital			500,000
Issued Share Capital			350,000
RESERVES			
Retained Profit			163,400
LONG-TERM LIABILITIES			
Long-term Loan			65,000
Capital Employed			578,400

Question

H '96 II 3

The following trial balance was extracted from the books of Daly Ltd on 31 May 1996. The Authorised Share Capital is 300,000 €1 ordinary shares.

You are required to prepare the company's trading, profit and loss and appropriation accounts for the year ended 31 May 1996 and a balance sheet as at that date.

	DR €	CR €
Purchases and Sales	86,000	194,000
Wages	24,000	
Debtors and Creditors	26,300	11,600
Equipment	84,000	
Import Duty	7,350	
Sales Returns and Purchases Returns	3,500	4,200
Rent	16,400	
Insurance	6,200	
Interest Receivable		5,600
Cash	1,700	
Bank	7,950	
Motor Vehicles	75,000	
Premises	130,000	
Reserves (Profit and Loss Balance)		16,000
Opening Stock (1/06/95)	13,000	
Ordinary Share Capital 250,000 €1 ordinary shares		250,000
	481,400	481,400

You are given the following information as at 31 May 1996.

Closing Stock €15,500
Import Duty Due €450
Rent Prepaid €800
Dividend Declared 12%
Depreciation: Equipment 15%; Motor Vehicles 20%

Questions

H '06 I A3(b)

A firm's Profit & Loss Account for the year showed a Net Profit of €65,000. It was later discovered that insurance prepaid of €1,500 was left out.

Tick-(✓) the appropriate box below to show the correct net profit figure:

(i)   Net Profit of €66,500   ☐
(ii) Net Profit of €63,500   ☐
(iii) Net Profit of €65,000   ☐
(iv) Net Profit of €62,000   ☐

H '06 II 4(a)

H '05 II 4   H '03 II 4   H '01 II 4

H '04 II 4   H '02 II 2   H '00 II 3

Your revision notes

●●●Learning Objectives

Learn how to:

- assess the final accounts of a business, using suitable measures (compare with history, industry, ideal)
- prepare a report on findings

Understand:

- return on; share capital/capital employed
- gross profit mark up
- gross/net profit margin
- working capital ratio; acid test ratio
- rate of stock turnover
- period of credit given/received
- solvency
- rate of dividend

Tip
Tick each one off when you feel confident that you know it.

The final accounts (Trading, Profit and Loss and Appropriations Account and Balance Sheet) of a business show what has happened in a business over a period of time, but we need to be able to tell if the company has performed well or badly.

 **Understand**

Who is Interested in the Performance of a Company?

Shareholders/Investors
What profit did the company earn and what dividend is to be paid?

Banks
Will the firm be able to repay a loan?

Creditors

If I sell to this firm on credit, will I get paid on time (or at all)?

Management

Comparing profit with other companies and with previous years helps them to make decisions.

Employees/Trade Unions

Is the company healthy and can it pay good wages?

Revenue Commissioners

Make sure the company pays the proper tax on its profits.

Limitations of Final Accounts

- final accounts only give information about a particular year
- balance sheets only show the position of a business on a particular date/day
- final accounts and balance sheets do not take into account changes in the economy and things such as inflation or economic growth
- final accounts and balance sheets do not reveal details about staff morale, strikes, customer loyalty, etc
- assets will be shown at cost. They might be worth more now (e.g. most buildings have increased in value over the past number of years)

Analysing the Accounts

If a company makes a profit of €100,000, is that good or bad? The answer depends on a number of things.

We need to calculate some ratios and then compare them to see how well the company has done. The ratios can be compared with:

1 Last Year
2 Other companies in the same business.
3 A Standard

The ratios can be grouped under five headings:

1 Profitability

These ratios look at the profit the company made compared with the size of the company, measured in different ways.

Name	Formula	Answer	Compared with	Good/ Bad
Percentage Mark Up	$\dfrac{Gross\ Profit}{Cost\ Of\ Goods\ Sold} \times \dfrac{100}{1}$	Per cent %	Last year Other Companies	The bigger the % the better
Gross Profit Margin (Percentage)	$\dfrac{Gross\ Profit}{Sales} \times \dfrac{100}{1}$	Per cent %	Last year Other Companies	The bigger the % the better
Net Profit Margin (Percentage)	$\dfrac{Net\ Profit}{Sales} \times \dfrac{100}{1}$	Per cent %	Last year Other Companies	The bigger the % the better
Return on Capital Employed	$\dfrac{Net\ Profit}{Capital\ Employed} \times \dfrac{100}{1}$	Per cent %	Last year Other Companies Interest from the bank	The bigger the % the better
Return on Share Capital	$\dfrac{Net\ Profit}{Issued\ Share\ Capital} \times \dfrac{100}{1}$	Per cent %	Last year Other Companies Interest from the bank	The bigger the % the better

2 Liquidity

This is the ability of the company to pay its debts when they are due.
Overtrading is when current liabilities are greater than current assets
(i.e. negative working capital).

Name	Formula	Answer	Compared with
Current Ratio (Working Capital Ratio)	Current Assets : Current Liabilities	Ratio ? : 1	2 : 1 is the ideal
Quick Ratio (Acid Test Ratio)	(Current Assets – Closing Stock) : Current Liabilities	Ratio ? : 1	1 : 1 is the ideal

If the ratio is above 2:1 or 1:1, the company has money tied up in current
assets that might be better invested in machinery or something similar.

If it is below 2:1 or 1:1, then the company may not be liquid.

> **Tip**
>
> The current ratio and quick ratio are always written as 'Something : One'.

3 Solvency

If total assets are greater than outside liabilities, the company is said to be *solvent.*

If outside liabilities are greater, the company is *insolvent* and must not continue in business.

Name	Formula	Answer	Compared with
Solvency Ratio	Total Assets : Outside Liabilities	Ratio X : 1	If less than 1 : 1 the firm is insolvent

Total Assets = Fixed Assets + Current Assets
Outside Liabilities = Current Liabilities + Long Term Liabilities

4 Activity

These ratios show how busy the company has been over the year.

Name	Formula	Answer	Compared with	Good/Bad
Stock Turnover	$\dfrac{Cost\ Of\ Goods\ Sold}{Average\ Stock}$	Times	Other companies in the same business	Higher rate of turnover is better
Creditors' Payment Period	$\dfrac{Creditors}{Credit\ Purchases} \times \dfrac{365}{1}$	Days	Debtors' Payment period	Days taken by you to pay a bill
Debtors' Payment Period	$\dfrac{Debtors}{Credit\ Sales} \times \dfrac{365}{1}$	Days	Creditors' Payment Period	Days taken by your debtors to pay you

If the debtors' payment period is longer than the creditors' payment period, this means that you pay your bills faster than you are paid yourself.

> **Tip**
>
> Average Stock = (Opening Stock + Closing Stock) ÷ 2

5 Dividend Policy

The dividend is the profit paid out to the shareholders. We saw in chapter *33* that any dividend is usually given as a percentage of issued share capital.

Name	Formula		Answer	Compared with	Good/Bad
Rate of Dividend	$\dfrac{Dividend\ Paid}{Issued\ Share\ Capital}$	$\times \dfrac{100}{1}$	Per cent %	Interest paid by a bank	Higher rate of dividend is better

How to

To Help Decide How Well a Business Has Performed

You need to be able to:

1 Calculate
2 Compare
3 Comment (This is often done by writing a report)

Sample Question

Examine the final accounts and balance sheet of St Paul's Ink Ltd, set out below, for the year 2009 and calculate the following:

1 Gross mark up percentage
2 Gross profit percentage
3 Net profit margin
4 Return on capital employed
5 Return on share capital
6 Current ratio
7 Quick ratio
8 Solvency ratio
9 Rate of stock turnover
10 Debtors' payment period
11 Period of credit given
12 Rate of dividend

Trading, Profit and Loss and Appropriations Account for St Paul's Ink Ltd for the year ended 31-10-09

Credit Sales		640,000
Opening Stock	16,000	
Credit Purchases	440,000	
	456,000	
Closing Stock	14,000	
Cost of Goods Sold		442,000
Gross Profit		198,000
Total Expenses		72,000
Net Profit		126,000
Dividend		40,000
Retained Profit		86,000

Balance Sheet for St Paul's Ink Ltd as at 31-10-09

Fixed Assets		
Premises		452,000
Current Assets		
Stock	14,000	
Debtors	40,000	
	54,000	
Current Liabilities		
Creditors	50,000	
Working Capital		4,000
Net Total Assets		456,000
Financed By		
Issued Share Capital		320,000
Reserves		86,000
Long Term Liabilities		50,000
		456,000

Solution

1	**Gross Mark Up Percentage** $$\frac{\text{Gross Profit}}{\text{Cost Of Goods Sold}} \times \frac{100}{1}$$	$$\frac{198,000}{442,000} \times \frac{100}{1}$$	44.80%
2	**Gross Profit Percentage** $$\frac{\text{Gross Profit}}{\text{Sales}} \times \frac{100}{1}$$	$$\frac{198,000}{640,000} \times \frac{100}{1}$$	30.94%
3	**Net Profit Margin** $$\frac{\text{Net Profit}}{\text{Sales}} \times \frac{100}{1}$$	$$\frac{126,000}{640,000} \times \frac{100}{1}$$	19.69%
4	**Return on Capital Employed** $$\frac{\text{Net Profit}}{\text{Capital Employed}} \times \frac{100}{1}$$	$$\frac{126,000}{456,000} \times \frac{100}{1}$$	27.63%
5	**Return on Share Capital** $$\frac{\text{Net Profit}}{\text{Issued Share Capital}} \times \frac{100}{1}$$	$$\frac{126,000}{400,000} \times \frac{100}{1}$$	31.5%
6	**Current Ratio** Current Assets : Current Liabilities	54,000 : 50,000	1.08 : 1
7	**Quick Ratio** (Current Assets - Closing Stock) : Current Liabilities	(54,000 - 14,000) : 50,000	0.8 : 1
8	**Solvency Ratio** Total Assets : Outside Liabilities	(452,000 + 54,000) : (50,000 + 50,000)	5.06 : 1
9	**Rate of Stock Turnover** $$\frac{\text{Cost Of Goods Sold}}{\text{Average Stock}}$$	$$\frac{442,000}{\frac{1}{2}(16,000 + 14,000)}$$	29.47
10	**Creditors' Payment Period** $$\frac{\text{Creditors}}{\text{Credit Purchases}} \times \frac{365}{1}$$	$$\frac{50,000}{440,000} \times \frac{365}{1}$$	42 days
11	**Period of Credit Given** $$\frac{\text{Debtors}}{\text{Credit Sales}} \times \frac{365}{1}$$	$$\frac{40,000}{640,000} \times \frac{365}{1}$$	23 days
12	**Rate of Dividend** $$\frac{\text{Dividend Paid}}{\text{Issued Share Capital}} \times \frac{100}{1}$$	$$\frac{40,000}{320,000} \times \frac{100}{1}$$	12.5%

Sample Question

H '02 II 6b

The directors of Bingo Ltd., Sligo supplied the following figures for the years 2000 and 2001.

	2000	2001
	€	€
Sales	530,000	560,000
Net Profit	120,000	110,000
Current Assets	36,000	24,000
Current Liabilities	16,000	32,000
Capital Employed	380,000	460,000

Assume you are Pauline Willis, Management Consultant, Double Entry Road, Wexford.

Prepare a report, on today's date, for the directors of Bingo Ltd, comparing and commenting on the performance of the business over the two years, 2000 and 2001. Use the following three ratios in comparing performance:

Net Profit Percentage; Return on Capital Employed; Current Ratio. (34)

Solution

To: The Directors
Bingo Ltd
Date: 12/06/2002
From: Pauline Willis
Management Consultant
Double Entry Rd
Wexford

Terms of Reference: Assess the performance of the company over the two years, 2000 and 2001, using three ratios.

Findings

Ratio	2000	2001
Net Profit Ratio	22.64%	19.64%
Return On Capital Employed	31.58%	23.91%
Current Ratio	2.25 : 1	0.75 : 1

Conclusions

Overall, the business is not doing well. The net profit ratio and the return on capital employed have both fallen during the year. The current ratio has fallen below the recommended 2:1 and the company will probably experience difficulty paying bills as they fall due. The company may close if urgent action is not taken.

I am available to discuss any of the above

Signed

Pauline Willis

Pauline Willis
Management Consultant

Questions

Try these other questions

H '94 II 5

Assume you are Joe Cronin, Financial Consultant, of 10 Cork Road, Waterford. Study the final accounts and balance sheet of King Ltd, Waterford, set out below, for the years 1993 and 1994. Prepare a report, using today's date, for the shareholders of King Ltd, comparing the performance of the company in the two years under the following three headings.

i) Profitability   ii) Liquidity   iii) Dividend Policy

1993		1994	
Trading Profit and Loss and Appropriations Accounts for year ended 31-05-93		Trading Profit and Loss and Appropriations Accounts for year ended 31-05-94	
	€		€
Sales	140,000	Sales	270,000
Less Cost of Sales	84,000	Less Cost of Sales	108,000
Gross Profit	56,000	*Gross Profit*	162,000
Less Expenses	44,600	Less Expenses	135,500
Net Profit	11,400	*Net Profit*	28,500
Less Dividends	1,400	Less Dividends	10,500
Reserves	10,000	Reserves	18,000

Balance Sheet as at 31-05-93			Balance Sheet as at 31-05-94		
Fixed Assets		105,000	Fixed Assets		95,000
Current Assets		20,000	Current Assets	30,000	
Less Current Liabilities	30,000	-10,000	Less Current Liabilities	15,000	15,000
		95,000			110,000
Financed By			*Financed By*		
Ordinary Share Capital		70,000	Ordinary Share Capital		70,000
Reserves		10,000	Reserves		28,000
Long Term Loan		15,000	Long Term Loan		12,000
		95,000			110,000

Questions

Paper I Section A questions		Paper II Questions	
H '01 I A 19	H '03 I A 18	H '05 II 6	H '02 II 6
H '02 I A 20	H '03 I A 7	H '04 II 5	H '04 II 4
H '02 I A 17	H '04 I A 3		
H '02 I A 4	H '05 I A 20		
	H '06 I A 14		

Your revision notes

CHAPTER 36

Club Accounts

●●●Learning Objectives

Learn how to:

- prepare the accounts from given figures
- prepare a treasurer's report

Understand:

- the differences between the final accounts of a club and a limited company
- (analysed) receipts and payments account
- income and expenditure account
- balance sheet

Tip

Tick each one off when you feel confident you know it.

Understand

A club is a not-for-profit organisation run for the benefit of its members. Officers are elected by the members to run the club.

Duties of Club Officers

Chairperson	Secretary	Treasurer
Runs the club	Maintains club correspondence	Collects subscriptions and issues receipts
Sets the agenda for meetings	Sends out notices of meetings	Makes all lodgements and payments for club
Chairs the meeting	Takes notes at meetings and keeps minutes	Keeps financial records
Puts motions to a vote	Makes minutes available to those who attend the meeting	Prepares final accounts
Has casting/ deciding vote if meeting can't decide		Reports to AGM, including financial recommendations

Club Terms

Annual General Meeting: A meeting held once a year at which all members of the club may attend. Each officer will report to the members.

Agenda: A list of items to be discussed at a meeting.

Minutes: A written record of the decisions taken at a meeting. They may also contain the main points of any discussions.

Club accounts are very similar to business accounts. The main difference is in the terms used.

In a Business	In a Club
Cash Book	Analysed Receipts and Payments Account
Profit and Loss Account	Income and Expenditure Account
Capital	Accumulated Fund
Net Profit	Excess of Income over Expenditure
Net Loss	Excess of Expenditure over Income
Balance Sheet	Balance Sheet
Trading Account	Trading Account

NB Although a club is a not-for-profit organisation, it may earn some income from trading (e.g. a bar, shop or canteen). If this is the case, a trading account showing gross profit is prepared. Only this profit (or loss) is included in the income and expenditure account

How to

Accounts of a Club

The accounts kept by the treasurer are:

1. Analysed Cash Book (Day to Day)	2. Receipts and Payments Account (Annual Summary)
3. Income and Expenditure Account	4. Balance Sheet

Tip

The income and expenditure account may include a trading account if the club has a bar, shop or similar.

1 Analysed Cash Book/Analysed Receipt and Payments Book

(The same as the cash book for a business or household)

Dr Receipts   Cr Payments

Analysis columns based on club requirements.

Sample Question

Tory Drama Society kept a record of its finances in an analysed cash book. On 1 January 2007, it had an overdraft of €379 in the bank. The following transactions took place during the year:

Date	Particulars	Cheque No	€
Jan 4	Paid Eblana Ltd for advertising	134	193
Feb 29	Lodged membership subscriptions		400
Mar 9	Paid for stock for snack shop	135	112
Apr 2	Deposit receipts from Easter concert		1,342
Apr 17	Paid for rental of scout hall	136	170
May 5	Paid Bus Éireann for bus hire	137	156
Jun 20	Lodged raffle receipts		933
Jul 18	Purchased costumes and equipment	138	1,800
Aug 13	Lodged receipts from sales from snack shop		173
Sept 14	Purchased stock for snack shop	139	40
Oct 17	Paid for rental of scout hall	140	170
Nov 22	Lodged receipts from November concert		715
Dec 10	Lodged receipts from snack shop		74

Record the above transactions for the year in the club's analysed cash book using the following money column headings:
Debit (Receipts) Side: Raffle, Concert, Snack Shop, Subscriptions.
Credit (Payments) Side: Advertising, Snack Shop, Rent, Travel, Equipment.
Complete and balance the analysed cash book on 31 December 2007.
(22 marks)

Solution

Debit Side

Date 1996	Particulars		Total Bank	Raffle	Concert	Snack Shop	Subscriptions
Feb-29	Subscriptions		400				400
Apr-02	Easter Concert		1,342		1,342		
Jun-20	Raffle		933	933			
Aug-13	Refreshments		173			173	
Nov-22	November Concert		715		715		
Dec-10	Refreshments		74			74	
			3,637	933	2,057	247	400
01/01/1997	Balance	b/d	617				

Credit Side

Date 1996	Particulars	Chq. No.	Total Bank	Advertising	Snack Shop	Rent	Travel	Equipment
Jan-01	Balance	b/d	379					
Jan-04	Eblana Ltd	134	193	193				
Mar-09	Refreshments	135	112		112			
Apr-17	Scout Hall	136	170			170		
May-05	Bus Éireann	137	156				156	
Jul-18	Costumes & Equipment	138	1,800					1,800
Sep-14	Refreshments	139	40		40			
Oct-17	Scout Hall	140	170			170		
Dec-31	Balance		617					
			3,637	193	152	340	156	1,800

2 Receipts and Payments Account

Prepared annually.

Uses the headings from the analysed receipts and payments account.

Sample Question

Tory Drama Society kept a record of its finances in an analysed cash book. On 1 January 2007, it had an overdraft of €379 in the bank. The following extracts show the totals of the cash received and lodgements book and the cheque payments book for the year ended 31/12/07.

Analysed Cash Receipts and Lodgements Book

Date 2007	Particulars	Total Bank	Raffle	Concert	Snack Shop	Subscriptions
31/12/2007	Total	3,637	933	2,057	247	400

Analysed Cheque Payments Book

Date	Particulars	Total Bank	Advertising	Snack Shop	Rent	Travel	Equipment
31/12/2007	Total	2,641	193	152	340	156	1,800

Assume you are the treasurer finalising the accounts for the AGM, prepare:
A) i) A Receipts and Payments account (13 marks)

Solution

Receipts and Payments Account for Tory Drama Society for the year ended 31/12/07

	Raffle	933	39,083	Balance	b/d	379
	Concert	2,057		Advertising		193
	Snack Shop	247		Snack Shop		152
	Subscriptions	400		Rent		340
				Travel		156
				Equipment		1,800
			21/12/07	Balance	c/d	617
		3,637				3,637
01/01/2008	Balance	617				

Tip

Remember

The analysed cash receipts and lodgements book is exactly the same as the debit side of the analysed cash book in the previous example.

The analysed cheque payments book is exactly the same as the credit side of the analysed cash book in the previous example.

Tip

Balance b/d on the credit side is an overdraft.
Balance b/d on the debit side means the club has money in the bank.

---

3 Income and Expenditure Account

Based on the receipts and payments account.

Note the following:

The income and expenditure Account **does** include:

1 Income earned during the year (subscriptions, sponsorship) add income due at the end of the year (subscriptions due) subtract income prepaid at the end of the year (subscriptions prepaid)

2 Expenses paid during the year (wages, repairs) add expenses due at the end of the year (wages due) subtract expenses prepaid at the end of the year (insurance prepaid)

3 Depreciation is an expense which does not appear in the receipts and payments account, but should be included here

The income and expenditure account **does not** include:

1 Opening and closing cash and bank balances
2 Purchase and/or sale of fixed assets

Tip

Any trading account will need to be prepared **before** the income and expenditure account.

Sample Question

Based on H '97 I B3a(ii)

Using the information in the receipts and payments account from the previous sample question and the following information available at the end of the financial year:

Subscriptions Due	€45
Rent Due	€160
Advertising Prepaid	€69
Depreciation of	€545
Snack Bar stock 01-01-07	€146
Snack Bar stock 31-12-07	€134

Assume you are the treasurer finalising the accounts for the AGM, prepare:

i) Snack Bar trading account, and
ii) An income and expenditure account for the year ended 31/12/07 (22 marks)

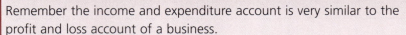

Tip

Remember the income and expenditure account is very similar to the profit and loss account of a business.

Only the snack bar profit/loss will be shown in the income and expenditure account.

Solution

Snack Bar Trading Account of Tory Drama Society for the Year ended 31/12/07

Snack Sales			247
Less Cost of Sales			
Opening Stock		146	
Snack Purchases		152	
Cost of Goods Available		298	
Closing Stock		134	
Cost of Goods Sold			164
Gross Profit			83

Income and Expenditure Account of Tory Drama Society for the Year ended 31/12/07

Income			
Subscriptions		400	
+ Subscriptions Due		45	445
Concerts			2,057
Raffle			933
Snack Bar Profit			83
			3,518
Expenditure			
Advertising	193		
- Advertising Prepaid	69		
Travel		156	
Rent	340		
+ Rent Due	160	500	
Depreciation		545	1201
Excess of income over expenditure			2,317

255

4 Balance Sheet

Prepared annually. The layout is exactly the same as a company balance sheet except for the 'Financed by' section, where:

1 Capital is called accumulated funds
2 Profit and loss is called excess of income over expenditure (or surplus)

Sample Question

The treasurer of Tory Drama Society has been taken ill and you have been asked to help prepare accounts for the Annual General Meeting next week. Using the following account balances, prepare:
A balance sheet as at 31/12/07. (15 marks)
You have been given the following account balances.

Equipment	4,200	Excess of Income over Expenditure	2,317
Furniture	2,500	Subscriptions Due	45
Accumulated Fund (01/01/97)	3,517	Rent Due	500
Advertising Prepaid	69	Snack Bar Stock	134

Furniture is depreciated by 5% per annum
Equipment is depreciated by 10% per annum

Solution

Balance Sheet for Tory Drama Society as at 31-12-07			
Fixed Assets	Cost	Depreciation	NBV
Equipment	4,200	420	3,780
Furniture	2,500	125	2,375
	6,700	545	6,155
Current Assets			
Canteen Stock		134	
Subscriptions Due		45	
		179	
Current Liabilities			
Rent Due		500	(321)
Total Net Assets			5,834
Financed By			
Accumulated Fund (01-06-91)			3,517
Add Excess income over Expenditure			2,317
			5,834

Treasurer's Report

The treasurer's report is presented at the AGM. It lets the members know how the club is financially.

Sample Question

Prepare a report for presentation to the members of Tory Drama Society using the accounts above. (15 marks)

Solution

Tory Drama Society
Treasurer's Report

To: Society Members   14 January 2008
From: Dick Evans

Please find attached with this the final accounts and balance sheet of the club.

Body of Report
1. The profit from the snack bar was €83 as shown in the trading account.
2. The club had a surplus of €2,317 last year, mainly due to the concerts.
3. €45 in subscriptions is still owing at the end of the year.

I am available to discuss this report if required.

Signed
Dick Evans

Questions

Try these other questions

H '95 I B 4

The following information was presented by the treasurer of Liosnacree Hurling Club for the year ending 31 December 1994.

	€
Cash in Hand 01-01-94	430
Payments	
Travel Expenses	2,470
Light & Heat	520
Insurance	760
Purchase of Lawnmower	6,500
Raffle Prizes	580
Receipts	
Membership Fees	1,200
Gate Receipts	3,450
Raffle Income	7,600

Additional Information:

i) Membership fees due on 31-12-94   €450
ii) Insurance prepaid on 31-12-94   €140
iii) Lawnmower to be depreciated by 10% each year.

   A Prepare:

      i) A receipts and payments account, and (11marks)
      ii) An income and expenditure account for the year ending 31-12-94 from the information above. (15 marks)

   B

      i)   How much cash did the club have on 31-12-94?
      ii) What is an agenda for a meeting?
      iii) List **three** duties of a club treasurer.
      iv) Explain the term **depreciation**. State one cause of depreciation. (14 marks)

Questions

Short Questions

H '96 I A 18

Tick (✓) the correct answer below.
The capital of a club is called:

Excess of Income	☐
Net Assets	☐
Accumulated Fund	☐
Liquid Capital	☐

H '06 II 6(c)

Long Questions

H '06 I B 2(a)	H '01 I B 5
H '05 I B 2	H '00 I B 4
H '04 I B 2	
H '03 I B 3	
H '02 I B 5	

●●●**Learning Objectives**

Learn how to:

● prepare the accounts from given figures

Understand:

● operating statement
● balance sheet
● the differences between the final accounts of a service firm and a limited company

> **Tip**
>
> Tick each one off when you feel confident that you know it.

A service firm is a business which supplies a service rather than selling a product, e.g. doctors, plumbers, travel agents, hairdressers.

Like any other firm, the final accounts show how the business has performed over time, i.e. did they make a profit or a loss and what assets and liabilities the company had on a certain date.

 **Understand**

The Accounts

1 The *analysed cash receipts and lodgements book* and *analysed cash and cheque payments book* (*analysed cash book*) show the cash receipts and payments for the year.

These are identical to those of a business or a club (*See Chapter 27*).

2 The **operating statement** shows the profit or loss for the year. Like a club, a service firm does not trade (buy and sell) as its main business, but it may sell goods as a part of the service. For example, a hairdresser may also sell shampoos and conditioners.

3 The **balance sheet** lists the assets and liabilities of the firm at the end of the year. This follows exactly the same layout as the balance sheet of a trading firm or a club.

Sample Question

It's a Snip Ltd is a hairdressing salon. They prepare an operating statement and a balance sheet at the end of each year. The following trial balance was taken from the books on 29-02-08.

You are required to prepare:

(i) An operating statement for the year ended 29-02-08 (10 marks)

(ii) A separate trading account for haircare products for the same period (5 marks).

(iii) A balance sheet as at 29-02-08 (15 marks).

Trial Balance as at 29-02-08	DR €	CR €
Sales income from:		
Haircuts and treatments		116,405
Haircare products		3,900
Rates	5,200	
Insurance	12,000	
Wages	39,420	
Light and Heat	9,940	
Purchases of haircare products for resale	2,100	
Stock of haircare products (01-03-07)	800	
Bank overdraft		2,955
Premises	85,000	
Cash on hand	8,700	
Equipment	19,650	
Debtors and Creditors	3,300	2,850
Ordinary Share Capital (60,000 €1 shares)		60,000
	186,110	186,110

Stock of haircare products on 29-02-08 was €650

Tip

Although the first thing you are asked to do is to prepare the operating statement, the trading account needs to be prepared first.

Solution

Haircare Products Trading Account of It's a Snip Ltd for the Year ended 29/02/08

Haircare Product Sales			3,900
Less Cost of Sales			
Opening Stock		800	
Haircare Product Purchases		2,100	
Cost of Goods Available		2,900	
Closing Stock		650	
Cost of Goods Sold			2,250
Gross Profit			1,650

Operating Statement of It's a Snip Ltd for the Year ended 29/02/08

Income			
Haircuts and Treatments			116,405
Haircare Products Profits			1,650
			118,055
Expenditure			
Rates		5,200	
Insurance		12,000	
Wages		39,420	
Light and Heat		9,940	
Total Expenditure			66,560
Net Profit			51,495

Balance Sheet for It's a Snip Ltd as at 29-02-08			
Fixed Assets			
Premises			85,000
Equipment			19,650
			104,650
Current Assets			
Stock of Haircare Product		650	
Debtors		3,300	
Cash on Hand		8,700	
		12,650	
Current Liabilities			
Creditors	2,850		
Bank Overdraft	2,955	5,805	6,845
Total Net Assets			111,495
Financed By			
Ordinary Share Capital (60,000 €1 shares)			60,000
Reserves			
Net Profit			51,495
			111,495

Your revision notes

Question

Paige Turner is a bookbinder. She prepares an operating statement and a balance sheet at the end of each year. The following trial balance was taken from her books on 31-10-10.

Trial Balance as at 31-10-10

	DR €	CR €
Sales income from		
Bindings and Repairs		228,005
Antique Books		4,700
Rates	5,200	
Insurance	7,200	
Wages	39,420	
Light and Heat	8,840	
Purchases of Antique Books for Resale	1,100	
Stock of Antique Books (01-11-09)	800	
Bank Overdraft		3,555
Premises	185,000	
Cash on Hand	3,600	
Equipment	9,650	
Debtors and Creditors	3,300	2,850
Ordinary Share Capital (25,000 €1 shares)		25,000
	264,110	264,110

Stock of Antique Books on 31-10-10 was €650
You are required to prepare:
(i) An operating statement for the year ended 31-10-10. (10 marks)
(ii) A trading account for the year ended 31-10-10. (5 marks)
(iii) A balance sheet as at 31-10-10. (15 marks)

Questions

H '99 II 3   **H '06 I B2(6)**

●●●Learning Objectives

Learn how to:

- prepare the accounts from given figures
- prepare a report on farm accounts

Understand:

- reasons for keeping farm accounts
- income and expenditure
- the balance sheet

> **Tip**
>
> Tick each one off when you feel confident that you know it.

- a farm is a business and needs to keep accounts like any other business:
  - ○ to find out if a profit or loss has been made
  - ○ to find out which part of the farm business is most profitable
  - ○ to calculate tax liabilities
  - ○ to collect information for government or EU grants
  - ○ to give information when applying for a loan.

Understand

The Accounts

1 The *analysed cash receipts and lodgements book* and *analysed cash and cheque payments book* (*analysed cash book*) shows the cash receipts and payments for the year.

These are identical to those of a business (*See Chapter 27*).

Tip

Remember, the *analysed cash receipts and lodgements book* and *analysed cash and cheque payments book* (*analysed cash book*) do not show prepayments, accruals or depreciation.

2 The *income and expenditure account* shows the profit or loss for the year.

Tip

The income and expenditure account *does not* include:
● opening and closing cash and bank balances
● purchase or sale of fixed assets (e.g. machinery*)*

3 The *balance sheet* lists the assets and liabilities of the farm at the end of the year
This follows exactly the same layout as the balance sheet of a trading firm.

Tip

Remember

Adjustments			
Expense Due	Add Current Liability	*Expense Prepaid*	Subtract Current Asset
Income Due	Add Current Asset	*Income Prepaid*	Subtract Current Liability

Sample Question

Bill and Pat Jackson keep accounts for their farm. They have supplied you with the following annual records and ask you to prepare:
An income and expenditure account for the year ended 31-12-08 and a balance sheet as at that date.
Income for the year ended 31-12-08

Income for the year ended 31-12-08	€
Milk	17,890
Sheep	5,300

Expenditure for the year ended 31-12-08	€
Wages	12,470
Rent	990
Insurance	3,200
Vet Fees	1,300

Assets as at 31-12-08	€	Liabilities as at 31-12-08	€
Land	150,000	Loan	150,000
Buildings	120,000	Creditors	3,500
Debtors	4,500	Bank Overdraft	1,900
Cash	500	Capital	158,766
Machinery	14,000		

You are given the following additional information:
 i) Insurance Prepaid   €425
 ii) Rent Due   €198
 iii) Machinery to be depreciated at 10%

Solution

Income and Expenditure Account for B & P Jackson for the Year ended 31/12/08			
Income Milk			17,890
Sheep			5,300
			23,190
Expenditure Wages		12,470	
Rent	990		
+ Rent Due	198	1,188	
Vet Fees		1,300	
Insurance	3,200		
- insurance prepaid	425	2,775	
Depreciation		1,400	
Total Expenditure			19,133
Net Profit			4,057

Balance Sheet for B & P Jackson for the Year ended 31/12/08			
Fixed Assets	Cost	Depr.	N.B.V.
Land	150,000	---	150,000
Buildings	120,000	---	120,000
Equipment	14,000	1,400	12,600
	284,000	1,400	282,600
Current Assets			
Debtors		4,500	
Insurance Prepaid		425	
Rent Due		198	
Cash		500	
		5,623	
Current Liabilities			
Creditors	3,500		
Bank Overdraft	1,900	5,400	223
Total Net Assets			282,823
Financed By			
Capital			158,766
Net Profit			4,057
Long Term Liabilities			
Loan			120,000
Capital Employed			282,823

Questions

Try these other questions

H '97 II 6

A) List **four** reasons why farmers should keep accounts.

B) Dinny and Teasie own a farm in Wicklow and have a balance of €3,500 in the bank on 1 May 1997. They ask you to help them write up their analysed cash book (analysed receipts and payments book) for the month of May 1997 from the data below:

Use the following money column headings:

Debit (Receipts) side: Bank; Sheep; Cattle; Grants; Other.

Credit (Payments) side: Bank; Feed; Fertiliser; Cattle; Vet; Expenses.

2/5/1997	Paid the Vet	Cheque No. 11	€130
5/5/1997	Sale of Sheep	Receipt No. 2	€1,600
8/5/1997	Purchased Calves	Cheque No. 12	€1,500
12/5/1997	Received EU Grant		€2,000
13/5/1997	Purchased Fertiliser	Cheque No. 13	€400
16/5/1997	Purchased Feed	Cheque No. 14	€200
19/5/1997	Paid ESB	Cheque No. 15	€165
21/5/1997	Sold Cattle	Receipt No. 3	€3,000
24/5/1997	Paid Insurance	Cheque No. 16	€460
27/5/1997	Received a Loan		€12,000
28/5/1997	Paid Contractor	Cheque No. 17	€18,500
30/5/1997	Purchased Tractor	Cheque No. 18	€5,700
31/5/1997	Sold Cattle	Receipt No. 4	€6,900
31/5/1997	Sale of Vegetables	Receipt No. 5	€145

C) Dinny and Teasie were advised that they should join a local co-operative.
i) Explain briefly what a co-operative is, and give an example of one.
ii) State **three** advantages of joining a co-operative.

H '06 I 7

Outline two reasons why farmers prepare farm accounts:

(i)
_____
_____

(ii)
_____
_____

●●●Learning Objectives

Learn how to:

- recommend a computer system for use in the home
- recommend a computer system for use in a business
- state the functions of: operating system; word processing; spreadsheet; database; the internet and e-mail

Understand:

- input devices, output devices, hardware, software
- uses of computers in the home (accounts, letters, entertainment, communications)
- uses of computers in business (accounts, communications, sales & marketing, CAD/CAM)

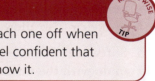

Tip

Tick each one off when you feel confident that you know it.

Understand

Information Technology means machines used to store, process and transmit information.

Main Components

Hardware refers to the computer and other things that work with a computer.

Software refers to the instructions to make the hardware work.

1 **Input Devices:** Are used to give information and instructions to the computer.
- a scanner lets the computer 'read' pictures and documents
- bar-code scanner
- a keyboard lets the user type instructions and information
- a mouse lets the user move things around the 'desktop'
- a modem allows the computer to connect to the internet and get information

2 Processing: The 'brain' of the computer

The Central Processing Unit (CPU) does all the calculations and follows the instructions given. Processors are usually measured in Gigahertz (GHz). Higher GHz means a faster and more powerful computer.

3 Storage: Memory may be measured in Megabytes (Mb) or Gigabytes (Gb) or Terabytes (Tb). 1000Mb = 1Gb, 1000Gb = 1Tb

There are two main types of memory.

a) **ROM** (Read Only Memory): This is where the computer stores the basic instructions on how to work. The information in ROM cannot be changed.

b) **RAM** (Random Access Memory): This is where the computer stores information it needs to do the current task. Information can be stored or deleted from RAM at any time. Anything stored here is lost when the computer is switched off.

Because information in RAM is lost when the computer is switched off, it is necessary to save any information you will need again.

This can be done internally (in the hard drive) or externally.

The most popular forms of external storage are floppy disc or CD-ROM (Compact Disc - Read Only Memory).

4 Output Devices: These give information to the user.
- monitor (Visual Display Unit = VDU) is the screen you look at
- printer puts the information onto paper (makes a *hard copy*)
- a modem also allows the computer to send information to the Internet

5 Software: These are the instructions for the computer that tell it what to do with the information.

a) Operating System – The basic instructions for how the various input and output devices work together (e.g. Windows, Linux, OSx).

b) Word processor – For producing written documents. It allows you to change the appearance before printing it. Most word processors also include a spellcheck which will correct the most common spelling mistakes (e.g. MS Word).

c) Spreadsheet – For handling numbers, making graphs and charts, etc. Many people use a spreadsheet for keeping their accounts and budgets (MS Excel, Lotus).

d) Database – Data is a number of facts. A company would have data on customers (e.g. names and addresses of customers and what they buy). A database program will let them examine the data and find customers in the same area or those who buy the same products (e.g. MS Access, Foxpro).

e) Graphics – For creating or modifying pictures.

f) Mail Merge – A combination of a database and a word processor. It allows a list of names and addresses to be combined with a standard letter so that each person gets a letter with their own details without having to type out a new letter each time.

g) CAD/CAM – Computer Aided Design, Computer Aided Manufacture. Helps a business design products and control the manufacturing process. For example, a company that designs and makes furniture can help decide how to lay out the pieces to cut them out with the least waste, and then control the saw as it does the cutting.

Networks and the Internet

If one or more computers are connected so they can share devices or information, this is called a network.

Often a network will have a special computer called a server controlling how and when and what the computers share.

The Internet is a worldwide network of computers to which anyone can connect with a computer, a modem and a phone line.

Information passes quite slowly over a phone line. Broadband is an improved technology which allows the information to pass many times faster.

E-mail is a system for sending letters and other information from one computer to another through the Internet. You need an e-mail account and the e-mail address of the other computer to send an e-mail.

The *World Wide Web (WWW)* is a library of pages of information on a huge range of subjects. It can be searched using a search engine (Google, Yahoo etc.).

How to

Factors to Consider When Buying a Computer System

- purchase cost of the computer, the software, and any input and output devices.
- other running costs
- is the computer powerful enough to do what is expected?
- will it help the business/household?
- what software will be needed to perform the task expected?
- what training will be required?
- how long will the equipment last?

Operating Costs for a Computer System

- purchase cost
- depreciation
- cost of finance
- electricity, paper, ink

- internet connection
- maintenance

Use of Computers and IT

In the Home
- word processing, e-mail, WWW, budgeting and accounts
- games consoles (Playstation, X-box)
- online banking

In Business
- filing, word processing, accounts
- CAD/CAM
- stock control by connecting the bar-code scanner at the till to the computer
- automatic ordering
- e-mail and internet selling
- some hotels and airlines allow customers to book rooms or flights
- computer-based training

Questions

Try these other questions

H '96 I A12

Write a brief note on:
i) Mail Merge   ii) RAM

H '98 I A3

Tick (✓) the correct answer.
Which of the following computer programs can best be used for filing information?

Spreadsheet   ☐   Database   ☐
Word Processing   ☐   Graphics   ☐

H '99 I A 11

In relation to information technology, what do the following initials stand for?
a) ROM   b) RAM

H '00 I A

What do the following initials stand for in relation to computers?
a) IT
b) PC
c) CAD
d) VDU

H '97 I B 6

Sharon Burke is the owner of a small business. She has little knowledge of computers, but has recently done some desk research on them and their workings. She is confused with some of the terminology/terms used and requests your help and advice.

a) i) Explain what is meant by the underlined words above.

ii) Explain the difference between computer hardware and software. (10 marks)

b) What is the function of computer input devices? (9 marks)

c) Name two important technical factors (excluding price) which a computer owner should take into consideration when selecting a computer program for a computer (6 marks).

d) What types of computer programs are required to undertake the following tasks?

i) Information storing

ii) Budgets and accounts (6 marks)

H '98 II 4

Robo Ltd of 23 High St, Gort, County Galway, is considering computerising its sports equipment manufacturing business. Robo Ltd expects to start exporting its sports equipment worldwide in 1999. It requires advice on computer systems and sources of finance.

Assume you are Chip Micro, Computer Consultant, 10 Disk Rd, Dublin 2.

Prepare a report for the directors of Robo Ltd, on today's date, setting out the following:

three factors to be considered when deciding on a computer system.

three types of computer software suitable for business (32 marks).

H '03 I A 2

H '04 I A 19

H '01 I B 6

H '05 I A 1

H '0 I B2(b)

H '02 I B 3b

The examination for Higher Level Junior Certificate Business Studies is divided into two papers, both examined on the same day. These papers are worth a total of 400 marks. Each paper examines different parts of the course and it will help you to prepare for the examination if you know what to expect.

Paper One

Time: 2½ hours
240 marks

Section A (80 Marks)

Twenty short questions from all parts of the course. Answer **all** questions.

Section B (160 Marks)

Six questions from chapters 1–14, 18–21, 35–36, and 38–39 of this book. You must answer **four** questions.

Question 1 is always a Household Budget Question (budget or comparison).

If you learn final accounts of a Private Limited Company you need only learn the few differences for the others. A club makes a surplus, not a profit; a Service Firm has an Operating Statement not a Trading Account, and so on.

Timing

2½ hours broken down as follows:

10 minutes – read the entire paper and pick your questions.
30 minutes – Section A (this will help you settle down).
25 minutes – do your best long question.
25 minutes – do next best question.
25 minutes – do next best question.
25 minutes – do next best question.
10 minutes – reread your answers. Correct any errors you find.

Watch your time. If you aren't finished a question and 25 minutes is up, go on to the next question. You can come back if you have time to spare later, but most students score about half the marks they will get in a question in the first 10 minutes.

You probably won't have time to spare but if you do, there is no harm in attempting a fifth question.

Paper Two

Time: 2 hours
160 marks

Six questions from chapters 15–17, 21–34, 37 and 39 of this book.
You must answer **four** questions.
Question 1 is always a question on Books of First Entry, Ledgers, credit and cash transactions.

Few students attempt Question 1, as it can take a lot of time. It is best avoided if you cannot work very quickly.

Questions on Paper Two tend to have a bookkeeping element to them somewhere. If you study chapter 30, this shouldn't present any great problems.

Timing

2 hours broken down as follows:
10 minutes – read the entire paper and pick your questions.
25 minutes – do your best long question.
25 minutes – do next best question.
25 minutes – do next best question.
25 minutes – do next best question.
10 minutes – reread your answers. Correct any errors you find.

Preparing for the Examination

The sooner you revise something after learning it for the first time the more of it you will remember. Aim to revise within twelve hours. That's what homework is for. Revise again within one day, one week and one month. After that it will be easy to refresh your memory.

When studying, you can highlight in the text book or you can make your own notes. If you make your own notes you have to use more of your brain. You read it. You think about how to write it down in as few words as possible. You write it. All this helps you to remember.

Once you have made study notes, you should avoid going back to the text. The next time, study your notes, and make notes on that. Every time you do this you get better at remembering the material and your notes get shorter so revision gets faster.

Don't forget you don't have to use full sentences; you can use arrows, pictures and spider diagrams (mind maps) like this:

Spider Diagram

Sitting the Examination

Read the questions carefully and answer the question asked. Underline the key points in the question and be sure you don't miss out.

Not only are you allowed to use a calculator in the examination, but you should do so. There is no point in losing marks for making silly mathematical errors that you would not normally make.

Show your workings. Even if you get the wrong result, by showing your calculation process you will pick up some marks.

Follow all instructions given on the paper (N.B. headings on analysis columns, using + and - in budget comparison, etc).

Were you asked for a letter, a memo, a report? Marks are awarded for using the correct layout.

In all questions keep your work as tidy as possible. If the examiner can't read it, you won't get the marks for it.

Keep an eye on timing. In the long questions, give 10 minutes for every 16 marks.

Up to 4 marks go for putting appropriate titles on the Final Accounts. Make sure you put the titles on.

Study Plan

Date			
Time			
Section to be revised			

Date			
Time			
Section to be revised			

Date			
Time			
Section to be revised			

Date			
Time			
Section to be revised			

Date			
Time			
Section to be revised			

Date			
Time			
Section to be revised			

Night before exam

Sections to be revised

Study Plan

Date			
Time			
Section to be revised			

Date			
Time			
Section to be revised			

Date			
Time			
Section to be revised			

Date			
Time			
Section to be revised			

Date			
Time			
Section to be revised			

Date			
Time			
Section to be revised			

Night before exam	
Sections to be revised	

i 18506355

Your revision notes